BreadTube Se Imperialism

CALEB T. MAUPIN

BreadTube Serves Imperialism

Examining The New Brand of
Internet Pseudo-Socialism

CONTENTS

Acknowledgements

I would like to thank Arthur Porter for his cover design, Denise Rampulla for her proof-reading and Jason Ross for his layout. I also want to thank everyone who helped contribute to this book with research and moral support over the past two years as I have been subject to a widespread personal smear campaign. Special thanks to Brenton Lengel, Peter Coffin, Daniel Burke, Dakotah Lily, George Ehrhardt, Ramiro Funez, Nathan Rich, Peter Coffin, Justin Simmons, Lily Goldklang, Joe Gale, Charlotte Forrester, Kiki Dewar, Garland Nixon, Dr. Wilmer Leon, Paul Shepard and others who have offered ideological and political support.

Introduction: The Capitalists Fight With One Another...

The capitalists fight with one another
To corner the market and divide up the world
Their quest for maximum profit
Is the cause of war and puts us on the dole
Their greed leads them into a crisis
Which they try to resolve with a more fascist state
Our struggle is against the whole capitalist system
So strike at the fascists as well as the cuts
— Cornelius Cardew, Lords of Labour

The events of January 6, 2021 will go down in history. The images of supporters of President Donald Trump and adherents of the QAnon Conspiracy Theory bursting into the US Capitol building shook the world. While US media presented it as simply an example of the criminal and violent nature of Trump supporters, to any observer with an astute political understanding, it showed much more than that. The extent to which FBI informers and other infiltrators were involved in helping the events to happen as they did has not yet been fully revealed. Such an occurrence was only allowed to happen because deep divisions exist within the US power structure. Within the circles of wealth and power, the intelligence agencies, and the military, there are serious divisions. The pandemic, the bumbling government response at local and federal levels, and the resulting economic fallout has only exacerbated those differences.

US society is in a deep crisis. The crisis is rooted not in multiculturalism, a lack of patriotism, or a lack of virtue signaling and "woke" sentiments, but in the fundamental problems of capitalism. Capitalism, the system of production organized for profit, is reaching a breaking point. A prolonged crisis of overproduction, spawned by the computer revolution, has made the longstanding problem of workers' competition with machines and poverty resulting from abundance far more deadly. Workers are suffering, the economy is stagnating, unrest is rising, and the influence of the United States around the world is in decline.

Divisions in the Ruling Class

The trend which Karl Marx described in his pamphlet *The Eighteenth Brumaire of Louis Napoleon* in which one section of the capitalist class seeks to suppress other sections in an attempt to stabilize society and liquidate the crisis, is very much alive. The Obama administration, in an alliance with ExxonMobil, the Rockefellers, and the Silicon Valley tech giants, attempted to carry out strategies put forward by the Council on Foreign Relations, and introduce measures to better control the US economy and strategically roll back the influence of Russia and China. Trump, aligned with capitalists like Betsy DeVos, Sheldon Adelson, Mike Lindell, the fracking corporations and military contractors, took moves to push back against these moves. The goal was to maintain a more libertarian economic model, and secure the profits of those who lost out from Obama's maneuvers.

In the 1980s, the US ruling class seemed to be in a state of near unity and the US economy was strong. Ronald Reagan remarked, "We are all friends after six o'clock" when speaking of the elected officials in Washington, DC. The events on January 6th indicate, pretty clearly, the opposite state of affairs.

The January 6th events reminded many of the events of August 11th and 12th, 2017 in Charlottesville. A crowd of white nationalists and conservatives assembled for a torch lit march, and the following day held a public demonstration to oppose the removal of a monument to the Confederacy. At the demonstration on August 12th, left-wing activists mobilized to counter the racists. Scuffles took place, and a white supremacist activist plowed his car into a crowd of leftists, killing Heather Heyer. A police helicopter also crashed, killing two state troopers.

In other writings, such as my book *Kamala Harris and the Future of America*, I have provided extensive analysis of the divisions within the US ruling class. I focus on how these divisions have evolved over the course of the last decades and what the various factions want. This text will focus on another aspect of the conflict.

The Marxist composer Cornelius Cardew penned these lyrics describing the process of capitalist decay: "The capitalists fight with one another to corner the markets and divide up the world, their quest for maximum profits is the cause of war and puts us on the dole. Their greed leads us into a crisis, which they try to resolve with a more fascist state, our struggle is against the capitalist system, so strike at the fascists as well as the cuts."

It has long been understood that as the capitalist crisis emerges, the various factions in the ruling class form political movements to serve them. These political movements target one section of the capitalist class on behalf of the other, while also mobilizing against revolutionary forces that seek to overthrow the capitalist system.

British intelligence officer Frank Kitson described the practice of forming "Counter-Gangs" in Kenya to fight against the Land and Freedom Army. These were pseudo-revolutionary groups that collected intelligence and helped the British empire to defeat the Mau Mau uprising. Kitson later pioneered the British intelligence strategy of arming Protestant fanatics to target the Irish Republican Army during the 1980s.

William S. Lind, the Pentagon strategist and military analyst, has developed the concept of Fourth Generation Warfare, in which "non-state actors" are utilized by great powers in their efforts to undermine rivals.

Endless pages have been written about how the right-wing faction of US capital is utilizing white nationalists, QAnon, Libertarians, the Tea Party, and other rightists as a "counter-gang" of "non-state actors" to fight on their behalf. However, very little has been written about what is obviously retaliation from the rival faction. The internet culture of "Social Justice Warriors" and the emergence of a group of pseudo-leftist internet voices called "BreadTube" is an attempt to counter the influence of right-wing voices among the US population, with the covert backing of the rival faction of imperialists.

Countering the right-wing is certainly a noble effort as the racism, destructive economic ideas, and delusional conspiracy theories coming from the Trump faction are certainly problematic. However, the "BreadTube" current are loyal servants of the more liberal faction among the imperialists, and as such they have engaged in a second mission. In addition to countering the right-wing faction, the second task the BreadTube milieu has engaged in is an effort to purge left-wing circles of all illiberal, anti-imperialist voices and to some extent, all voices that are genuinely anti-capitalist. In order to transform leftism into nothing but lockstep servitude of their preferred faction among the ruling class, they seek to equate Marxist-Leninists and 21st Century Socialists with the far-right.

Lessons from the 1930s

BreadTube's efforts are reminiscent of the efforts by the social democrats following the Russian Revolution. During the 1920s and up until the mid 1930s, the various parties that had once made up the Second International, said "Our main enemy is on the left." In the name of opposing Communism, the Social Democrats, including the Socialist Party of America, sought to have Communists banned from labor unions, suppressed by the government, and thrown in prison.

In Weimar Germany, the Social Democratic Party formed its own militia to suppress the German Communist Party. In events like the infamous "Bloody May" (Blutmai) of 1929 in Berlin's Wedding district, police officers and others associated with the Social Democratic Party killed 33 Communists while suppressing an uprising.

In response, Communists across the world accused social democrats of being "social fascists." British communist theoretician R. Palme Dutt composed an important book entitled *Fascism and Social Revolution*, arguing that social-democrats ultimately served the same purpose as Italian Fascisti, brutally suppressing communists and stabilizing capitalism.

In 1935, the Soviet Union faced the threat of Nazi invasion, and global politics had significantly shifted as a result of Hitler's seizure of power. The Communists of the world re-oriented to building a People's Front. They aligned with social democrats. In the lead-up to the Second World War, social-democrats dropped much of their anti-communist fanaticism and embraced Communists as anti-fascist allies. The various "People's Front" alliances, including the Roosevelt Coalition in the United States, won many great victories for working people, and set the stage for the defeat of fascism.

During the 1920s, German Communists fought against social democrats who raised the slogan "our main enemy is on the left." The anti-communist violence of social democrats eventually set the stage for the Nazi takeover in 1933.

Many observers have noted the historical irony of Communists and Social-Democrats, who literally killed each other in Germany, France, Britain and elsewhere, joining arm in arm shortly afterward. However, circumstances had changed. The realignment resulted in a convergence of interests. The Social-Democrats faced the threat of extermination from fascists who were aligned with industrial capitalists and militarists. Communists also faced extermination from fascists and the Soviet Union realized a Nazi invasion was inevitable. This common interest in defeating fascism brought the two trends together during the Popular Front era and the Second World War.

More Dangerous Than Social Democracy

While many lessons can be learned from this period, it must be noted that much of BreadTube's ideology is fundamentally more dangerous to those who seek to overturn capitalism than social democracy was during the 1920s and early 1930s.

While the Social Democrats of the 1920s and 30s opposed the Soviet Union and the Communist Parties, they accepted the overall Marxist analysis of capitalism. Social Democrats worked in labor unions and sought to increase the living standards of working people. Social Democrats believed history was moving forward and that technological progress was a good thing. Social Democrats sought, through gradual reform, to eventually establish a society where the means of production operated according to a rational central plan.

The prevailing voices on BreadTube do not share these goals with Marxists. The prevailing BreadTube view is that the living standards of working people in the United States and throughout the world are too high, and that consumption must be reduced. BreadTube voices generally argue that advocating for living standards to increase or analyzing society in terms of wage workers and capitalists is an ideological crime known as "Class Reductionism." BreadTube voices generally believe technological progress is an affront to mother nature, and that societies around the world that are kept in a state of deindustrialization and underdevelopment are more "pure" and "beautiful," close to some kind of spiritual ideal. BreadTubers generally reject the need for a centrally planned economy, but instead favor gradually transitioning to a profit-centered economy, where workers receive a share of the profits rather than a set hourly wage.

While Social Democracy in the 1920s and even today generally represents a watered down, pro-imperialist interpretation of Marxism, what BreadTubers believe in is fundamentally antithetical to Marxism. Marxism seeks to advance historical progress and create a society of vast abundance in which all inequality and the need for a state itself can fade away.

Contrarily, BreadTube seeks to roll back the wheels of history, reduce the human population, end growth, and restore humans to some kind of primitive state of existence deemed to be moral and sustainable.

While Social Democracy in the 1920s tended to oppose illegal activities and militant labor activism, BreadTube has taken the opposite extreme. BreadTubers tend to favor an escalation of street violence against the right-wing at a time when these forces are much better armed and have a much better organized base among the population. If the eventual escalation that BreadTubers seem committed to inciting were to occur, the result would most likely be a huge crackdown on all political activism by the state, if not an outright victory for the right-wing.

Furthermore, BreadTube often seems to almost incite lawless violence and hooliganism against Marxist-Leninists, 21st Century Socialists and Anti-Imperialists at the same time, that they call for mob violence against the right-wing. BreadTube is actively working to change the political discourse, labelling anti-war and anti-imperialist voices as "Red Browns" and "Nazbols," equating them with Nazis, and setting the stage of mob violence and state repression against them.

It may have been incorrect to label the social-democrats of the 1920s "social fascists" despite the fact that they advocated and engaged in violent repression against revolutionary forces. However, a much more explicitly fascist streak can be found in the BreadTube milieu. BreadTube's opposition to historical progress and growth evokes fascist Julius Evola's references to "The Demonic Nature of the Economy," and carries with it the genocidal legacy of eugenics and Malthusianism. BreadTube's fetishization of street violence and "action" over ideology, pushing left minded youth toward a premature violent confrontation, also parallels Mussolini's political trajectory as described in his autobiography. BreadTube's implied calls for violence and political repression of anti-imperialist voices certainly brings forth memories of the Nazi stormtroopers.

Whether or not BreadTube ideology constitutes a modern variant of fascism is not the focus of this book. BreadTube, after all, is merely an internet community engaging in propaganda work. The ties of BreadTube to the Antifa street fighters are most likely extensive but cannot be confirmed. So far, the actual violence against rival leftist voices has been rare, though cyber-bullying, intense harassment, and intimidation has not.

The purpose of this book is to debunk and expose the dangerous pseudo-leftism which BreadTube espouses. Genuine leftism and Marxism is the only way out of the crisis. The primitivist, worker-coop, "non-authoritarian" society BreadTubers advocate is not really achievable or desirable. The distorted and confused worldview BreadTubers promote ultimately serves the ultra-rich and globalist oriented factions of the capitalist class. While it has very little to do with Marxism, it is highly reminiscent of the occultist worldview of Marilyn Ferguson, a spiritual guru who was highly influential among American intelligence operatives. She served as spiritual advisor to Al Gore. This book will show that the BreadTube perspective is a mish-mash of old, deviant, pessimistic trends among the middle class utilized to combat the socialist movement.

Chapter One: What & Who is BreadTube? The Nature of the Counter-Gang

As of this writing, the current Wikipedia article on "BreadTube" opens by defining it this way: "BreadTube or LeftTube is a term used to refer to a loose and informal group of online content creators that provide editorial opinions and educational lectures from socialist, communist, anarchist, and other left-wing perspectives. BreadTube creators generally post videos on YouTube that are discussed on other platforms, such as Reddit. BreadTube creators are known to participate in a form of algorithmic hijacking. They will choose to focus on the topics discussed by content creators with far-right politics. This enables their videos to be recommended to the same audiences consuming far-right videos, and thereby expose a wider audience to their perspective."

This Wikipedia definition of BreadTube seems to almost confirm the thesis of this book, that BreadTube is an entity that is being utilized by the more powerful, liberal "globalist" wing of the western capitalist power structure to beat back the emerging right-wing opposition. It is worth examining a few of the major players in the BreadTube universe.

Natalie "Contrapoints" Wynn

Probably the most level-headed and articulate voice among the BreadTube community is Natalie Wynn, who uses the moniker Contrapoints. Natalie is a transgender college graduate from Arlington, Virginia. She studied at Berkeley College of Music, Georgetown University, and Northwestern University. Contrapoints has received advertising from mainstream US capitalist media, with outlets like the *New York Times* and *The New Yorker* giving their stamp of approval for her supposedly anti-capitalist rhetoric. The Southern Poverty Law Center, which equates Black Nationalists with Nazis and has pushed the narrative that anti-war leftists are "Red Brown" cryptofascists, has approvingly cited Natalie Wynn in their reports and praised her efforts.

Contrapoints has produced a number of high budget videos intended to refute right-wing ideas and urging the left to be more coherent in presenting an alternative message. While her content is certainly of a much higher quality than other BreadTubers and contains a level of intellectual depth and engagement most BreadTubers are incapable of, Contrapoints is not particularly loved. Contrapoints has been targeted viciously by her own BreadTube community, accused of "empathizing with bigots." Trying to understand right-wing views and why people adopt them is deemed an unforgivable crime by those who argue that only violence and cancel culture should be the response. This is a common viewpoint among BreadTube voices. Contrapoints, herself transgender, has been critical of the ideology advocated by much of the Trans movement, deconstructing some of the prevailing interpretations of what Transgenderism means. This has also made her the target of lengthy harassment campaigns.

Contrapoints generally puts forward the view that the US government has been infiltrated by a secret Nazi conspiracy and that the role of leftists is to protect the establishment by rooting out this conspiracy. Wynn urged leftists to vote for Joe Biden in a video where she compared advocating socialist revolution to suicidal ideation.

Harris "Bomber Guy" Brewis

Harris Michael Brewis, who uses the internet moniker "Hbomberguy," much like Contrapoints, devotes much of his content to debunking the views of right-wingers, not to promoting Marxism. Brewis is based in Britain and is a member of the Labour Party and a supporter of Jeremy Corbyn. His videos largely focus on debunking the claims of pick-up artists, flat earth conspiracists, and those who allege that soybeans reduce testosterone. He also comments on video games, movies, and other cultural topics.

One of Brewis' greatest achievements was a fundraising stream for the British Transgender advocacy and charity organization known as Mermaids. On this stream which continued for 57 hours and 48 minutes, Brewis was joined by US Representative Alexandria Ocasio-Cortez and Chelsea Manning, as well as a number of Hollywood actors such as Colin Mochrie and Mara Wilson.

Ian "Vaush" Kochinski

A video game playing child of wealth from Beverly Hills named Ian Kochinski has taken on the moniker "Vaush." He has been appointed by YouTube algorithms as the unofficial spokesperson for Marxist, Socialist, and Leftist thought. Vaush's father is Mark Kochinski, a figure in Hollywood who describes himself on LinkedIn as "director, visual effects artist, and supervisor with 20 years of experience in production."

In earlier years, Vaush used the moniker "IrishLaddie." He appeared on the streams of internet video game enthusiast Steven "Destiny" Bonnell to argue in favor of his interpretation of anarcho-communism. He eventually set up his own Twitch and YouTube channel on which to play video games and urge listeners to vote for Joe Biden. On his streams Ian often claims there is a secret Nazi conspiracy that has infiltrated the US government, misinterprets key Marxist concepts, equates critics of US foreign policy i.e. "Tankies" with Nazis, all while using excessive profanity. In the aftermath of the January 6th Capitol Riot, Vaush appeared to call for a mass totalitarian style "disappearing" of Trump supporters, tweeting out: "Democracies cannot coexist with these people. They disappear, or we all do."

Kochinski seems to have an odd fascination with pedophilia. In one debate he argued that purchasing a laptop computer was morally equivalent to purchasing child pornography. In other instances, he has argued for ending age of consent laws, though he has since claimed to have changed his position. The website *Drama Report* published an article on September 8, 2020, featuring claims from a former friend of Vaush who said he had admitted to her that he viewed child pornography and that she had reported him to the FBI.

Ian Kochinski has admitted that he did indeed sexually harass at least one woman while he operated under the moniker "IrishLaddie," sending them inappropriate messages, including statements about and photos of his genitals, and threatening to dox the woman if she went public about his behavior. Vaush has acknowledged and apologized for such actions. A large number of unconfirmed rumors about other sexual misconduct allegedly perpetrated by Vaush can be found online.

The personality of the 25-year-old indicates signs of narcissism and sex addiction. Some have speculated that his blatant rudeness and inability to comprehend other peoples' views indicates he may be on the autistic spectrum. Vaush seems to have a bigoted view of midwestern and southern Americans, viewing them as inferior rabble, not as sophisticated as he and his wealthy neighbors in Beverly Hills. In his perspective, the calls for economic justice from working people in the Rustbelt are "class reductionism" and "fascist populism."

Kochinski has lied excessively about this author, claiming he is a "literal Nazi" and that he supports US billionaire capitalists like Jeff Bezos, statements he clearly knows to be false. He also baited this author for allegedly being "anti-American," which is a very odd accusation for a supposed Marxist and Anarcho-Communist to make. In many streams it seems apparent that Vaush has "handlers" or "advisors" who are more familiar with Marxism than he is. Often Vaush will be seen stuttering his way through explaining concepts that he does not clearly understand, clearly quoting someone else, most likely an individual who learned the concept in an academic, not activist, setting.

In one embarrassing stream Vaush read aloud quotes from Mao Zedong, Lenin, and Marx, which he said justified support for the Democratic Party of the United States in the 2020 election. It became clear to many viewers that the list of quotes had been prepared by someone else, and that Vaush knows very little about Russian or Chinese history. However, this has not stopped this smug video game player from occupying the position of being the primary "Marxist" voice on the internet.

Vaush routinely quotes from Radio Free Asia and other US State Department propaganda outlets treating them as reliable sources of information, while deeming all media from anti-imperialist countries or putting forward an anti-imperialist perspective to be non-credible.

One of Vaush's favorite talking points is to accuse all who question US media allegations against China, Iran, Russia, and other anti-imperialist states of being the equivalent of Nazi Holocaust deniers. According to Vaush, if US media says that Saddam Hussein has weapons of mass destruction, or that the evil Spaniards have sunk the U.S.S. Maine, you must believe it. If you do not, you are the same as a Neo-Nazi and deserve to be beaten up by Antifa, if not "disappeared" in order to protect the great American "democracy."

"Socialism Done Left"

An individual using the name "Socialism Done Left" on Twitter and YouTube grabbed some widespread attention when it was revealed that they may not actually be a leftist at all.

According to an article published by *Vice News* on April 27th, 2021: "SocialismDoneLeft is a socialist YouTuber in the broad, loosely categorized group of YouTubers that's been dubbed 'BreadTube' by fans… While SocialismDoneLeft nominally pushes for progressive policies, the leaked Discord messages, which include dozens of overtly racist comments about Black people, antisemitic conspiracy theories, and Islamophobia, show that the public personas of some BreadTubers are at odds with what they say behind the scenes. It also has raised questions about whose side some of these streamers and YouTube personalities are really on. The messages, some of which SocialismDoneLeft has admitted to posting, apparently come from the YouTuber Destiny's Discord channel and were largely made in 2019."

While "Socialism Done Left" is a much less well known BreadTube personality, the revelations about them grabbed attention due to widespread suspicions about various BreadTube voices, their origins, and their sincerity. The *Vice* write-up goes on: "SocialismDoneLeft has since apologized for these messages on a Twitch livestream, saying that some of these statements were jokes made for 'shock humor,' and that he does not use this language anymore, three years later in 2021. He also said that in some cases he was mimicking the language of racists and emphasized that he doesn't find this language acceptable… Despite SocialismDoneLeft's apology, leftists on Twitter and elsewhere don't seem to be buying it, or at least they don't feel obligated to trust or listen to this person any longer."

The claim that such statements were intended as jokes doesn't seem to hold up when examining their context. The *Vice* report quotes one of the whistle-blowers who said: "Why the fuck are black people, Jewish people, and trans people always at the butt of these shitty 'jokes'?… Who were you parodying here? Punchline?"

It is worth noting that "Socialism Done Left" echoed the "Anti-Tankie" narrative equating leftists who do not echo US foreign policy rhetoric with the far right. It seems that inciting leftists against China was a primary focus of "Socialism Done Left" content, much of which has been removed in the aftermath of the leaked messages.

Matt "Thought Slime"

A Canadian comedian whose legal first name is "Matt" is one of the primary voices on the internet purporting to be an expert on Marxism and Anarchism. "Matt" identifies as non-binary, meaning they do not identify with either the male or female gender, and prefers to be referred to as "they" rather than "he" or "she." Matt uses the YouTube moniker "Thought Slime" and their video background features a green snot looking sludge.

Matt is essentially a cyberbully who wraps their comedy in pseudo-leftist ideology and 90s goth style edge-lordism. Matt seems to have had a very difficult life, something they frequently remind viewers of. Topics like suicide, depression, child abuse, bullying, and mental health are frequently discussed. After a failed comedy career, Matt turned to making movie reviews for YouTube and somehow seems to have stumbled into politics.

According to YouTube Wiki fandom, Matt's mother is Colleen Esteves, a convicted white collar criminal. According to a CBC report dated Sept 26, 2013, "Esteves worked with Human Resources and Skills Development Canada, as well as Service Canada, and deposited unauthorized funds into a joint account she held with her partner. The court was told during an earlier appearance that approximately $75,000 was deposited between January, 2007 and August, 2010. The court also heard that Esteves' partner had a gambling problem, and that he would inform authorities if she stopped taking money. He eventually did, when their relationship ended." The report states that Colleen Esteves "pleaded guilty to fraud and breach of trust by a public official."

No record exists of Matt ever being involved with any Anarchist or Communist organization, or any activism aside from their online comedy screeds. Matt's followers tend to target whoever Matt has chosen to unleash their rage on with absurd personal attacks and harassment. Matt routinely takes the statements that people make out of context, distorts opponents' positions, and makes statements that they most likely realize to be false. For example, Matt has claimed that this writer's father was a Wall Street banker and that this writer has never criticized the right-wing YouTube channel "PragerU," among other statements that are obviously inaccurate and could be debunked by a simple Google search.

Matt's videos tend to fixate on things like slime, feces, genitalia, and other things deemed to be ugly. Matt's channel is much like the Netflix show *13 Reasons Why* in that while it appears sympathetic to the mentally ill, it more or less encourages and enables people to fixate on their depressed, rageful, and suicidal feelings, wallowing in self-pity, anger, and hopelessness.

This begs a fair question: How many of Matt's mostly teenage and largely transgender audience have actually committed suicide after stewing with Matt for hours on their dark feelings? The answer is of course unknown.

Matt is kind enough to often provide a "trigger warning" in front of their more depressed or grotesque screeds.

Steven "Destiny" Bonnell

In addition to these prominent voices among the BreadTube universe, there are a couple of other individuals who are worth mentioning. While they are not all technically "BreadTubers" by definition, they are part of the sphere from which this crop of bizarre pseudo-leftist influencers have originated.

In 2011, a compulsive video game player from Nebraska quit his job as a carpet cleaner because he had figured out a method of making money entirely from playing the video game *Starcraft II*. Steven "Destiny" Bonnell had been live-streaming his playing of the game online, and made enough money from the advertising revenue that he was able to make a very sizable income and stop working elsewhere. This achievement made him quite famous among the internet video game community. For many gamers, being able to quit their jobs, give up going outdoors or making real social connections, and live entirely by gaming seems like a dream come true.

Already in Japan there has been widespread discussion of Hikikomori ("acute social withdrawal"), where technology enables young men to live as modern day hermits. Destiny is very much a celebrated hero among those attracted to such a lifestyle.

Destiny was known to make political comments during his video game livestreaming sessions. He generally classified himself as Libertarian. However, in the aftermath of Donald Trump's election in 2016, Destiny shifted toward advocating more social-democratic policies. He began having debates with white nationalists, conspiracy theorists, and others deemed to be the more dangerous segment of Trump's political base.

Destiny's sudden shift away from video games and cynicism with Libertarian individualism mixed in, toward the vague liberalism of the anti-Trump movement, was widely heralded in mainstream US media. An article from *Wired* published January 15, 2020 was entitled, "Can This Notorious Troll Turn People Away from Extremism?"

Destiny is not technically considered to be part of the BreadTube community. While he supported Joe Biden and advocated some left-wing policies like national healthcare, he explicitly rejects any form of Communism, Anarchism, or Marxism. Destiny is also known for having occasional right-wing turns. During the upsurge of Black Lives Matter protests in 2020, Destiny spoke with approval of right-wing activists and white supremacists who shot and killed protesters. Amid a rant condemning the property destruction of Black Lives Matter activists he proclaimed: "If that means like, white, redneck... militia dudes out there mowing down protesters who they can torch buildings at 10pm, then at this point, they have my blessing."

The BreadTube community was quick to denounce him for such comments, and he suffered a significant financial loss as many former patrons were horrified. It is a bit of an embarrassment for the BreadTube community that he has functioned as their Kingmaker. Ian "Vaush" Kochinski, for example, launched his career by being a frequent guest on Destiny's livestreams. Most of BreadTube's big names can be traced back to some connection with Bonnell.

It should be noted that the author of this book's entire introduction to the BreadTube universe came from an invitation to debate Steven "Destiny" Bonnell. Bonnell was entirely blown away by this writer's citing of actual data in defense of the existing socialist countries, and the debate resulted in a huge expansion of his social media following. Bonnell approached the debate in a very smug manner, assuming that "nowhere" had socialist central planning ever had economic successes. Amid the debate, at one point Steven sputtered out the phrase, "what does life expectancy prove?" revealing a darker, Malthusian undertone in his worldview.

Caleb "Faraday Speaks" Cain

Caleb Cain was made temporarily famous by a *New York Times* article published on June 8, 2019. The article is featured on the *New York Times* website with an intricate graphic and text that sounds almost like a movie trailer: "Caleb Cain was a college dropout looking for direction. He turned to YouTube. Soon he was pulled into a far-right universe, watching thousands of videos filled with conspiracy theories, misogyny, and racism. 'I was brainwashed.'"

The article seems, on its surface, to be a telling story of how an impressionable young man can be seduced by extremism and become a violent radical. The article opens with an account of him buying his first firearm. However, the actual details of Cain's story are quite disappointing.

Caleb Cain was a young man in West Virginia who had grown up in a conservative Christian family but became more liberal as he matured. According to his own account, he dropped out of college following some psychological problems, and began supporting himself by working at a warehouse. While working at the warehouse he had lots of time to listen to YouTube videos, and soon became a regular listener to Stefan Molyneux. Stefan is the "anarcho-capitalist" internet guru who is known to flirt with misogynist and racist ideas amid his overall libertarian perspective. After listening to Molyneux regularly, he also consumed content from other racist and far-right commentators.

Cain's story might be more compelling if from there he had become a terrorist or committed hate crimes, but it stops there. *The New York Times* narration has one expecting that Cain became a suicide bomber or mass shooter, or joined armed attempts to overthrow the government. However, he did none of this. The extent of Cain's "brainwashing" was listening regularly to right-wing voices online.

Cain eventually shifted his political views. A new girlfriend who had a more compassionate worldview and his changing life circumstances enabled him to be "deradicalize" and "unbrainwash" himself. Yet, in Cain's interviews he speaks as if he is repenting from the heaviest of sins. In one interview he says with deep regret that at one point he considered going to the Charlottesville protests in 2017, but decided not to.

After the advertising of the *New York Times* article, Cain launched his own YouTube channel, "Faraday Speaks," celebrating his status as a former extremist who had been deradicalized. However, the extent of Cain's "radicalism" was nothing more than listening to YouTube videos, becoming more distant with his family, and at one point considering going to a demonstration, but deciding not to.

Cain has collaborated with Destiny in efforts to combat the "extremism" that sucked him in. He has done interviews about how to "deprogram" ones' friends and relatives. But what exactly are they being deprogrammed from? Listening to videos online? Having political views that change with a new romantic relationship? Considering maybe going to a demonstration? Caleb Cain has made clear in interviews that he advocates for social media to censor and remove ideas he considers to be "conspiracy theories" in order to prevent others from being "brainwashed" as he was.

Caleb Cain's emergence as a minor figure in the BreadTube universe, initiated and promoted by mainstream media voices much like Destiny and Contrapoints, is almost comical. The nature of BreadTube as a poorly executed "deradicalization" effort by the most powerful factions among the imperialists is made quite apparent.

Dr. Steve Hassan

One figure who is definitely not part of the BreadTube universe, but certainly lurks in the background of discussions about "deprogramming" is psychologist Dr. Steve Hassan. Over the course of many decades, Hassan has carved out for himself the position as America's leading cult expert. His books on what he calls "Cult Mind Control" are widely circulated and he appears on CNN, MSNBC, and other TV outlets as an expert on the topic of brainwashing.

As a 19-year-old Steve Hassan was recruited into the Unification Church ("Moonies"). This is an anti-communist religious cult imported to the United States by the US Central Intelligence Agency to work against the growth of the Communist organizations on college campuses. In the 1970s many young people were involved in protesting the Vietnam War and in support of Black Liberation. College campuses were a hotbed of recruitment for the Revolutionary Union (now the Revolutionary Communist Party), Youth Against War and Fascism (youth wing of Workers World Party), the Young Workers Liberation League (now the Young Communist League, youth wing of the Communist Party USA), and other anti-imperialist and revolutionary organizations.

The Unification Church, a strange religious sect that worshipped a Korean pastor named Sun Myung Moon,

The rise of religious cults such as the Unification Church during the 1970s was intentionally fomented by US intelligence to counter the influence of Marxist-Leninist groups on college campuses.

had begun rapidly expanding in the United States during the 1970s. The group believed Moon was the new Messiah, sent to earth to unify the Christians of the world in a global crusade against Communism. Moon's cult had started in coordination with Korean intelligence as a way of "deprogramming" Marxist political prisoners and student activists. The Moonies became infamous for their predatory nature. They financially exploited members, demanding they hand over all their possessions, and spend each waking hour as unpaid laborers raising funds for the group.

Steve Hassan admits that the cult he spent roughly 2 years as an active member of was set up by American intelligence. In his appearance on the podcast of Jordan Harbinger he said: "Post World War Two, Korean war... South Korea was very unstable. North Korea is a version of what it is today... And some people in military intelligence in the United States decided, 'Well, the North Koreans are brainwashing, we need to create a program in South Korea to stabilize the regime.' They taught the South Korean President, 'You need to set up a Korean CIA, we'll help you' and they set up a re-education program for dissidents in South Korea, and they decided to use a front person, so it was not looking like a government operation, and it was the Moonies that were chosen to do that... The Moonies had, nobody knows why or how, the patents for manufacturing M16 Rifles and other American military hardware. Why? Because America was leaving Vietnam. Still the height of the Cold War, we have to stop the Commies. And then somebody said, 'Let's bring the Moonies to the United States and set up counter communist programs on college campuses' and that's where I got recruited… I was sent to fast for Nixon during Watergate, because God loves Nixon, God wants Nixon. The US government has never acknowledged the existence of these things. They don't want to talk about it."

As a young man rising up the ranks of the Moonies, Hassan eventually got into a car accident, and in the hospital his parents were able to lure him away from the group to their home where he was successfully "deprogrammed" by other former members. Eventually Hassan got involved with the Cult Awareness Network, an organization run by Ted Patrick.

Hassan worked with Patrick's organization, which charged lots of money to families for the service of kidnapping relatives believed to be in Moonies or other groups labelled as cults. Affiliates of the Cult Awareness Network are widely accused of having held these young legal adults against their will and "deprogrammed" them. Individuals who were "deprogrammed" by Patrick and his associates testified that the "deprogramming" sessions involved brutal interrogations, sleep deprivation, and the very techniques the cults were accused of using. Hassan has admitted that he was involved in "involuntary deprogrammings" but has not gone into detail about this.

Ted Patrick was convicted of kidnapping and false imprisonment in 1980 after he and other members of the Cult Awareness Network (the organization with which Steve Hassan was affiliated), kidnapped a 26-year-old waitress in Tucson, Arizona. Kidnapping and False Imprisonment are both very serious crimes, but Patrick only received a year in prison and a five thousand dollar fine. Patrick also faced charges in later years after he kidnapped an Amish woman whose husband disapproved of her joining a more liberal sect. These charges were ultimately dropped. The Cult

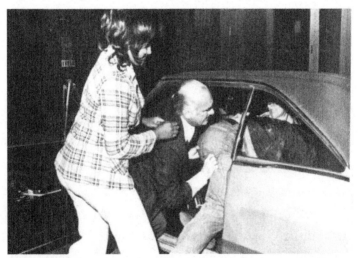

US media often highlights Steve Hassan as a cult expert, but rarely mentions his ties to the Cult Awareness Network, and accusations that he engaged in "involuntary deprogramming" i.e. kidnapping.

Awareness Network was eventually shut down in 1995 after a jury ruled that Jason Scott had his civil liberties and religious freedom violated when CAN affiliate Rick Ross kidnapped him and attempted to deprogram him. CAN was ordered to pay $1 million to Scott and ultimately went bankrupt.

Accounts from various individuals describe Hassan as being directly involved in the kidnappings. An individual named Arthur Roselle put forward a signed affidavit describing Hassan's methods. Roselle said he was "forcibly kidnapped by several men, imprisoned, hands and feet bound, with his hands tied behind his back so tightly they "were badly swollen and… the color of a bruise." Deprived of sleep for three days, he was not allowed to shave or wash and was denied all privacy, even when using the toilet… Hassan subjected him to methods the victim later described as brainwashing and mind control techniques. Hassan even threatened him with drugs if he did not recant his religious beliefs." Roselle described the experience, saying he felt like "a captured animal in a zoo." In his more recent books, Hassan has denounced kidnapping and forced deprogrammings, but he does not directly address most of the allegations about what he is alleged to have done with the Cult Awareness Network.

One would think that Hassan would be discredited due to his involvement in an organization that was widely reputed to have been involved in criminal activities. Hassan has not only avoided prosecution, but frequently appears on mainstream US television as a "cult expert." Hassan composed a book entitled *The Cult of Trump* in 2019, declaring that the US President was much like Reverend Sun Myung Moon and had "brainwashed" his supporters with hypnotic mind control methods.

Hassan made headlines in January of 2021 after an appearance on CNN in the aftermath of the events on Capitol Hill. Hassan said: "So, in studying all the thought-reform brainwashing models, I developed a BITE model of authoritarian control, and it basically talks about controlling behavior, information, thoughts and emotions to create a new identity that's dependent and obedient. And this is a radical personality change in the mental health literature. In the APA DSM-5 it's called the dissociative disorder, questioning of identity. And the bottom line is, all of America needs deprogramming because we've all been negatively influenced by Donald Trump." Congresswoman Alexandria Ocasio-Cortez echoed his calls for "deprogramming."

Hassan has been a mentor to Caleb Cain, and according to an unnamed source appears to be advising other members of the BreadTube community in their efforts to "deradicalize" Americans on the far right.

Hassan describes Donald Trump as the leader of a cult, and also refers to the internet conspiracy theory

QAnon as a cult, despite the fact that they do not fit his own criteria for what a cult is. Hassan's "BITE Model of Authoritarian Control" simply does not hold up. The behavior of QAnon adherents and Trump supporters is not restricted, and they are not told what information they can consume online or in the media; Trump supporters do not change their names or undergo hypnosis; the emotions of Trump supporters and QAnon are not subject to regulation. As bad as he is, Donald Trump is merely a demagogic politician with many fanatical supporters. As inaccurate and delusional as it is, QAnon is an internet conspiracy theory with all kinds of different interpretations among adherents. The political movement behind Donald Trump, or the internet conspiracy theories known as QAnon, have very little in common with the Unification Church. However, while media overlooks his own shady past, Steve Hassan has been given a platform to declare Trump and QAnon to be "a cult" and has suggested that mass "deprogramming" might need to take place.

Some other aspects of Steve Hassan are worth noting. While Hassan occasionally will admit that the Unification Church which he joined and feels horrifically victimized by was facilitated by the US government, he seems to hold no resentment against the CIA or the US government. In fact, in his anti-cult lectures he often makes statements like, "China is the biggest political cult in the world." He seems to have a particular vendetta against the Russian government, claiming that Russian President Vladimir Putin leads a political cult.

Hassan attributes much of his success to Robert Jay Lifton, a US Air Force psychiatrist who conducted research in Japan and Korea on US soldiers who had been converted to Communism in POW camps. Hassan admits that much of his understanding of "brainwashing" and "cult mind control" comes directly from Lifton, an individual who is very widely known to be involved with US military intelligence and its psychological operations against Communism.

Hassan's avoidance of prosecution for kidnapping, his celebration in mainstream media, his working of US Foreign Policy talking points into his cult lectures, his hinting at inside knowledge about the Unification Church's intelligence connections, and his close association with a high-ranking US military psychiatrist all indicate that Hassan is much more than a typical psychologist or anti-cult lecturer. Hassan appears to have "friends on the inside" who enable him to do what he does and see him as useful in carrying out their political goals. The same can be said for BreadTube, which appears to be some kind of cyber-age deprogramming operation aimed at the US right-wing, but also targeting legitimate Marxist-Leninists and anti-imperialists.

Counter-gangs and the Late Cold War

Understanding BreadTube's emergence as a brand of establishment-approved socialism while observing the lingering influence of a "deprogrammer" named Steve Hassan, forces us to discuss the 20th Century Cold War and how the Soviet Union and its allies were defeated. Below is an overview of the facts about how American intelligence was able to maneuver events toward the ultimate collapse of the Soviet Union. This will lay out the historical precedent for an entity like BreadTube and the purpose it serves, both domestically and internationally.

The Cold War between the United States and the Soviet Union began in 1946 after the Second World War and ended in 1991, when the Soviet Union was dissolved. The Cold War can be divided into two distinct periods.

The first period of the Cold War, beginning in the mid 40s and ending in the late 60s, involved American intelligence agencies and geopolitical strategists operating under the assumption that the enemy was Communism. The Truman doctrine of "containment" involved the United States building the NATO alliance, and seeking to unify the world against China, the Soviet Union, and other countries in which Marxist-Leninist parties had taken power. This period involved two massive US military interventions, one on the Korean Peninsula and the other in Vietnam. Both of these operations came at heavy cost to the United States in terms of human life, domestic morale, and international credibility.

During the Korean War, the world was shaken by the use of massive bombing of civilian targets by the US military. European allies and other international observers looked on in horror as US Army General Douglas MacArthur threatened to drop atomic bombs on China, without even the permission of the elected US President. Domestic opposition to the Korean War was limited due to McCarthyism and post-WW2 patriotism at home. However, among the soldiers on the battlefield it was a different story. Many American

At first only Communists like the W.E.B. Dubois Clubs and Youth Against War and Fascism protested the Vietnam War. However, by 1968, mass anti-war sentiments and a domestic political crisis had unfolded.

soldiers were disgusted by their orders to bomb civilians. Roughly 4,000 captured US soldiers signed confessions to war crimes and declared themselves to be Communist sympathizers in POW camps. This launched a wave of fascination with "brainwashing" in American media and among American intelligence researchers. At the war's conclusion, Korea remained divided and the Democratic People's Republic of Korea, which the USA had sought to eliminate, remained intact with a highly loyal population.

The setbacks experienced by the United States during the Korean War came back with an even greater vengeance during the Vietnam War. Protests against the war took place all across the world, with the Vietnamese people celebrated as peasant anti-imperialist heroes resisting the foreign occupiers. At home, protests against the war, combined with the rising unrest of the African-American community, resulted in a widespread episode of domestic unrest. In 1968, almost every major US city went up in flames following the murder of Dr. Martin Luther King, Jr., and campus anti-war protests became very popular. The communist factions of Students for a Democratic Society and the Black Panther Party emerged as explicitly Marxist-Leninist organizations seeking to overthrow US capitalism in alliance with Vietnam, China, Cuba, and the Soviet Union. Among the US army, defections, insubordination, and "fragging" of officers became widespread.

The United States was ultimately defeated in Vietnam, and as a result a new strategy for dealing with the Soviet Union and international communism emerged. This brought on the second stage of the Cold War, referred to as the "Late Cold War." Zbigniew Brzezinski, a Polish American academic, joined with strategist Henry Kissinger to establish the Trilateral Commission. The Trilateral Commission was a think tank funded by the Rockefeller family to reorient US foreign and domestic policy in light of the defeat of US forces in Vietnam and the widespread state of upheaval in the country at the time.

Zbiegnew Brzezinski was key in working with the Trilateral Commission to reorient US strategy in the aftermath of defeat in Vietnam. He focused on soft-power and manipulating Communists against each other.

Brzezinski's strategy for working against the Communists involved scaling back the use of massive bombing and long term military engagements, but instead utilizing proxy forces and exploiting the divisions that already existed among Communists.

Frank Kitson, the British intelligence officer who oversaw operations to defeat the Kenyan Land and Freedom Army, boasted of his use of "Counter Gangs" to defeat the Kenyan resistance to the British empire during the 1950s. Kitson directed the British Army to form groups of Black Africans and deploy them throughout Kenya. These "counter gangs" pretended to be Mau Mau liberation fighters, but were actually allies of the British. These forces collected intelligence, committed atrocities that could be blamed on the Mau Mau, sowed division among the Kenyan population, and ultimately enabled the British to defeat the insurgency.

Frank Kitson later went on to oversee British Military operations against the Irish Republican Army. In his work, he engineered a policy of arming Protestant extremists and enabling them to kill IRA members. A 2015 lawsuit was brought by Mary Heenan. Her husband was assassinated by Ulster Defence Association members in 1973. Her lawsuit alleged that Kitson was responsible for "the use of loyalist paramilitary gangs to contain the republican-nationalist threat through terror, manipulation of the rule of law, infiltration and subversion all core to the Kitson military doctrine endorsed by the British army and the British government at the time."

Brzezinski directed the United States to take a page from Kitson and begin setting up "counter gangs" around the world to fight Soviet aligned Communists, while the United States seemed apparently uninvolved. The first obvious use of the Kitson "counter-gang" strategy in the aftermath of the US defeat in Vietnam came in 1978 as the Kampuchea War. The Communist Party of Cambodia was overrun by a fanatical leader named Pol Pot and his followers. Pol Pot rejected industrialization and argued Cambodia could achieve

In order to defeat the "Mau Mau" Land and Freedom Army in Kenya, the British military developed the tactic of building "counter gangs."

full communism on the basis of the agrarian economy. Pol Pot attacked Vietnam, resulting in the Kampuchea War. China, arguing that the Vietnamese were acting as agents of "Soviet Social Imperialism," sent its forces to invade Vietnam in support of Cambodia.

It has later been revealed that Pol Pot, the crazed ultra-leftist who rejected basic principles of Marxism-Leninism and slaughtered hundreds of thousands of Cambodian and Vietnamese Communists, was in fact a covert puppet of the United States. Pol Pot had been educated in France, and the US government was providing him with guns and weapons in his fight against the pro-Soviet Communists in his homeland and against Vietnam.

Pol Pot and his allies represented a "counter-gang" much like those engineered by Frank Kitson in Kenya. The use of "counter-gangs" became a key staple of US strategic policy in the late Cold War.

Brzezinski bragged that he set up the "Afghan Trap" for the Soviet Union, creating a situation in Afghanistan where the Soviet Union would feel obligated to send in their military, and then arranging for Osama Bin Laden to build a global army of Wahhabi extremists from across the planet to fight them in the name of Islam.

In Angola, the United States armed a group called UNITA led by Jonas Savimbi, a literal cannibal and mass murderer, who claimed to be a Maoist Communist.

Savimbi's forces fought against the pro-Soviet ruling party of Angola, murdering civilians as well as Cuban and Angolan soldiers in a lengthy civil war. In Ethiopia, the United States armed Eritrean separatists to fight against the pro-Soviet Derg government.

In the Middle East, two anti-imperialist governments, the Islamic Republic of Iran and the Baath-Socialist Arab Republic of Iraq, were played against each other. The US government first supported Saddam Hussein in his invasion of Iran, and later the US government supported Iran in its fight against Iraq. There were mass deaths on both sides, among both fighters and civilians.

During this time many pro-Marxist college professors and writers in Europe received covert support from the US Central Intelligence Agency. They were carefully being nudged to push a more anti-Soviet brand of Marxism, focused on cultural issues rather than class struggle. The CIA boasts about the Congress for Cultural Freedom program, in which magazines like *Partisan Review, Encounter,* and *Der Monat,* were covertly funded to reorient Marxist thought among European intellectuals. In 1978 the Italian, French, and Spanish Communist Parties cut ties with the Soviet Union, and Brzezinski labelled them "EuroCommunists."

Counterculture-oriented religious groups like Rev. Moon's Unification Church (of which Steve Hassan was an ex-member), Transcendental Meditation, Tibetan Buddhism, and the Hare Krishna Movement, were deemed to be very useful by American intelligence in rolling back the influence of Communists among intellectuals and dissidents at home.

All of this covert manipulation of armed communist groups, socialist countries and leftist intellectuals culminated in overthrowing the Soviet Union in 1991. Many of the confused students who marched to overthrow the Marxist-Leninist governments in Eastern Europe did not think they were helping to bring in neoliberalism and the economic demolition of their homelands. They believed it was just to make a more "democratic" form of Socialism or "Socialism with a human face."

Decades later, in conditions where information travels much faster in the age of the internet, BreadTube appears to be yet another counter-gang. Like the Khmer Rouge, UNITA, the Congress for Cultural Freedom, or the various counterculture religious cults, it speaks in the name of left-wing sounding ideals. In reality, it is most likely serving one section of the American ruling elite and the intelligence agencies. Covert support is most likely being provided in order to enable the "algorithmic hacking" that has allowed BreadTube to flourish as the primary left-wing voice online, while waging a relentless campaign against others.

The important thing to remember about counter-gangs in the late Cold War is that they are generally not conscious deceivers. Some will read the above contents and believe that African Maoists, UNITA, Left-Wing Intellectuals, or the BreadTubers of 2021, are all "secret CIA agents" or some other crude interpretation. Nothing could be further from the truth.

There is no doubt that the fighters of UNITA, the Wahhabis who fought alongside Osama Bin Laden in Afghanistan, the intellectuals who pushed EuroCommunism, or even the BreadTubers of our time, legitimately believed in what they said and did. While they may be naive about the support they receive, what makes them useful proxies is their sincerity. Selecting certain ignorant and confused young people to be the voice of the movement and perhaps carefully nudging them to frame their rhetoric in a certain way is key. By rewarding them with patrons and clicks, the narrative can be carefully reinforced. A new "socialism" that is not anti-imperialist, not even genuinely anti-capitalist, but is very useful in containing and beating back the right-wing can be cultivated to serve imperialism.

Conclusion

An overview of the personalities, histories, and connections of various BreadTubers and affiliated personalities highlights certain similarities. None of them have any direct ties to any existing Communist, Anarchist, or Socialist activist groups, aside from perhaps Democratic Socialists of America. No record of actual activism as Marxists can be found when looking over their public history. Much like Alexandria Ocasio-Cortez, they seem to have appeared out of nowhere to suddenly become representatives of left-wing politics.

While they do not have ties to Marxist-Leninist or Anarchist activist groups, they do have apparent ties to the US power structure. Their work is celebrated in mainstream US media outlets. They are presented as a "safe" kind of leftism, and a needed counterbalance to the rise of Donald Trump.

Some of them have odd skeletons in their closets. Natalie Wynn's sudden rise to prominence; Vaush's shady history in relation to topics like child pornography and lack of charisma; the criminal conviction of Matt "Thought Slime's" mother and his fixation on topics like suicide and self-harm; Destiny's shift from Libertarian to Social Democrat, followed by his celebration of right-wing attacks on protesters; mysterious social media history of "Socialism Done Left"; Caleb Cain's celebrated status as an ex-right-wing extremist despite any real history of right-wing activism — all of these indicate that BreadTube has powerful allies who are using them to serve a purpose other than communist revolution.

Divisions within the capitalist ruling class are the natural outgrowth of an economic and social crisis such as the western world is currently experiencing. The alt-right and white supremacist groups put forward a toxic ideology that leads to hate crimes, mass shootings, and a justification for political repression. The existence of BreadTube as an entity pushed forward by elements within the deep state to defend the liberal order from right wing opposition is not really in itself a scandalous revelation. It is to be expected in times such as these.

However, in addition to demonizing the Trump movement and the various online currents aligned with it, BreadTube has another target. One thing that all these figures agree on is that China and Russia, and to some extent, Iran, Venezuela, Cuba, Vietnam, and Nicaragua are somehow toxic, totalitarian societies and it is the duty of western leftists to undermine and destabilize these countries. Vaush has been the most explicit in equating pro-Chinese Communists with Nazis, while celebrating the Hong Kong protesters who unfurl Pepe the Frog signs and Trump banners, but these sentiments are more or less prevalent throughout the entire BreadTube sphere. The narrative that somehow Trump supporters and QAnon are an extension of the illiberalism of the anti-imperialist bloc is also implied in much of BreadTube's material.

The main problem with BreadTube is not that it dissects the ideas of the far-right. This is largely a noble task, though it is sometimes very poorly executed due to the ideological limitations of those who avoid offending the liberal order. The main problem with BreadTube is that it is blatantly miseducating people and misrepresenting key concepts of Marxism, Socialism, and Communism.

BreadTube does not seek to make those exploring these concepts in a time of economic crisis into revolutionaries and anti-imperialists. Rather, they seek to make them into something much like they are, foot soldiers of the liberal order. They embolden the most powerful capitalists in their efforts to maintain power, beat back anti-imperialist states, and suppress unrest and rebellion at home.

Deconstructing the various misinterpretations and delusions presented by BreadTube in order to achieve this goal will be the purpose of the remaining pages of this book.

Chapter Two: Redefining Capitalism and Socialism

The name "BreadTube" is derived from a book published in 1892 by Anarchist Russian activist Peter Kropotkin. The book, entitled *The Conquest of Bread* and nicknamed "The Bread Book" is considered a primary text of "Anarcho-Communism." In the book, Kropotkin critiques both feudalism and capitalism, proposing a decentralized voluntarist collective society as the alternative.

Peter Kropotkin's ideas were fundamentally opposed to those of the Bolsheviks, who ultimately toppled the Czarist autocracy and later established the Soviet government in October of 1917. However, to discount Kropotkin and his ideas would be mistaken.

The Legacy of Peter Kropotkin

Kropotkin was born in the Russian aristocracy but from his youth, he became dedicated to the liberation of the Russian peasantry, who were brutally repressed. Kropotkin joined the International Workingmen's

Association (The First International), and worked alongside some of the most important revolutionary thinkers of the age. He spent years in prison for his beliefs, and took great risks. When the Russian Revolution occurred in 1917, Kropotkin embraced it as a positive development despite his criticisms and ideological differences. When Kropotkin died in 1921, Lenin personally approved a funeral procession of thousands of people to march in his honor. In 1957, the Soviet government named a subway station in his honor.

Kropotkin's influence spread well beyond Russia. Many Anarchists and leftist intellectuals across the world found his work and writings to be inspiring. Among those who were influenced by Kropotkin's work was a young man named Mao Zedong. Before joining the Chinese Communist Party at its founding congress in 1921, Mao Zedong was the leader of a Kropotkinist organization called the New People's Study Society, and many see the influence of Kropotkin popping up throughout Mao's life as a revolutionary and statesman.

The primary difference that Kropotkin had with the Bolsheviks was about who in Russian society should be the focus of the revolutionary movement. Kropotkin's focus was on the peasantry as the backbone of a potential revolution, while the Bolsheviks, as Marxists, viewed industrial workers as the sector of society where revolutionary work should be focused.

Kropotkin rejected some of Marx's economic ideas, arguing that the concept of surplus value was mistaken. As an anarchist, Kropotkin argued that a post-capitalist society could only be built voluntarily and that attempts to reform or seize political power were a waste of time. Kropotkin's vision was for the Russian peasantry to seize control of land themselves and begin growing crops cooperatively, much like German peasants had done during the event of 1524-1525. Kropotkin was an agrarian socialist rather than an industrial one.

Chapters 4-12 of his magnum opus for which the BreadTube community has taken its name are dedicated to laying an intricate vision of his ideal society of a decentralized, voluntary socialism with vast abundance. Kropotkin writes: "Citizens will be obliged to become agriculturists. Not in the same manner as peasants who wear themselves out, plowing for a wage that barely provides them with sufficient food for the year but by following the principles of market-gardeners' intensive agriculture, applied on a large scale by means of the best machinery that man has invented or can invent... They will reorganize cultivation, not in ten years' time, but at once, during the revolutionary struggles, from fear of being worsted by the enemy. Agriculture will have to be carried on by intelligent beings; availing themselves of their knowledge, organizing themselves in joyous gangs for pleasant work... when man invents and improves his tools and is conscious of being a useful member of the community."

Kropotkin's writing has an almost religious faith in the good intentions of human beings and their willingness to cooperate without coercion, combined with a gentle pacifism that fears the cruelty of authoritarian structures. He writes: "We shall see then what a variety of trades, mutually cooperating on a spot of the globe and animated by the social revolution,

BreadTube draws its name from an admirable Russian Anarchist named Peter Kropotkin. Kropotkin's organizing tactics among peasants were an influence on Chinese revolutionary Mao Zedong who organized the New People's Study Society before joining the Communist Party in 1921.

can do to feed, clothe, house, and supply with all manner of luxuries millions of intelligent men. We need write no fiction to prove this. What we are sure of, what has already been experimented upon, and recognized as practical, would suffice to carry it into effect, if the attempt were fertilized, vivified by the daring inspiration of the Revolution and the spontaneous impulse of the masses."

However, despite holding a vision of a voluntary society where all cooperate with each other in the absence of coercion, Kropotkin was not opposed to using force and violence to achieve his goals. The Anarchist organizations and networks he associated with throughout Europe advocated "Propaganda of the Deed," the use of bombings and assassinations in the hopes of sparking a rebellion among the wider population. How much Kropotkin was directly involved in such activities remains unclear, but it is clear that many people who were inspired by Kropotkin's teachings and worked with his organizations engaged in Left Adventurist Terrorism.

In 1916, most anarchists and revolutionary socialists were protesting and opposing the war between imperialist powers. Kropotkin published his "Manifesto of The Sixteen" that announced support for British and American imperialism in their war against Germany, Austria, and Turkey. This earned Kropotkin a large amount of scorn and was seen as a slap in the face and betrayal of the many socialists like Rosa Luxemburg and Eugene Debs, who went to prison for opposing the war.

Peter Kropotkin is a figure that is worthy of respect despite criticisms of his political line and actions. He was willing to make great sacrifices and take great risks on behalf of oppressed peasants and factory workers, and he did a great deal to put forward a vision of post-capitalist society that would resolve the injustices of the world. Marxists of course reject Left Adventurism and Terrorism along with idealistic fairy tales. They favor instead to build a mass movement of workers to seize control of the state, and create a rational, centrally planned economy to eliminate all scarcity, marching toward the ultimate goal of a stateless, classless world.

The fact that the BreadTube internet universe claims Kropotkin's legacy and presents itself as the main representative of not just Kropotkin's ideas, but all anti-capitalism in 21st Century America is deeply problematic. The intellectual laziness and shallow analysis presented by various BreadTube voices is a total disservice to his legacy, however complex it may be.

The Marxist Definition of Capitalism

The teachings of Karl Marx understand socialism to be a result of the innate human drive for progress and the expansion of productive forces. For most of humanity's existence, we lived as hunter gatherers in tribes. The first social revolution came with the domestication of animals and the growing of crops. The dawn of agriculture brought forth a new mode of production and a new set of social relations to correspond to it. Soon society was divided between landowners and slaves.

Eventually feudalism, a more efficient mode of production, replaced slavery. In the 1700s capitalism emerged in Europe as the mercantile classes replaced the kings and nobles, and industrial production replaced subsistence farming.

Capitalism resulted in the creation of two social classes, the bourgeoisie and the proletariat. The bourgeoisie are those who own the banks, factories, land, means of transportation and other centers of economic power, and operate them in order to make profits. The rest of society makes up another class, the proletariat, a class Marx described as: "the modern working class, developed — a class of laborers, who live only so long as they find work, and who find work only so long as their labor increases capital. These laborers, who must sell themselves piecemeal, are a commodity, like every other article of commerce, and are consequently exposed to all the vicissitudes of competition, to all the fluctuations of the market."

The interests of the capitalists who own the means of production and the workers who sell their labor power to capitalists are diametrically opposed. Capitalists seek to drive wages down and maximize their profits. As a result, workers form unions and organize strikes in the hopes of increasing their pay and bettering their conditions.

Capitalism is defined by Karl Marx and Friedrich Engels as a system in which the means of production are privately owned and operated to make profits for those who own them. Marx described capitalism as "the anarchy of production." Engels explained "For in capitalistic society, the means of production can only function when they have undergone a preliminary transformation into capital." Mao Zedong, the leader of the Chinese Communist Party, said that capitalism was a system of "Profits in command." **The capitalist system is defined as a system of production for profit.**

The capitalist is always looking to make production more efficient in order to increase his profits. As Marx explained, "The bourgeoisie cannot exist without constantly revolutionizing the instruments of production, and thereby the relations of production." The capitalist seeks to hire the least amount of workers, replace human labor with machines, de-skill jobs, and make human labor more easily replaceable, all in order to churn out more and more products for lower and lower cost. The capitalist seeks to increase his profit margin so those profits can be reinvested and his operations can expand only to make more profits, which can then be reinvested again. This is what Marx referred to as "The General Law of Capitalist Accumulation."

Driving down labor costs, however, has an unplanned side-effect. The purchasing power of workers is derived from the wages they are paid. In the drive to efficiently produce goods and maximize profits, the capitalist system is prone to cyclical crises of overproduction. The workers cannot afford to buy back the products they produce. The market becomes glutted with products that cannot be sold. As a result, prices drop, companies go out of business, and workers lose their jobs, because too much has been created.

Marx wrote in his text *The Poverty of Philosophy*: "From day to day it has becomes clearer that the production relations in which the bourgeoisie moves have not a simple, uniform character, but a dual character; that in the selfsame relations in which wealth is produced, poverty is also produced; that in the selfsame relations in which there is a development of the productive forces, there is also a force producing repression; that these relations produce bourgeois wealth; i.e., the wealth of the bourgeois class — only by continually annihilating the wealth of the individual members of this class and by producing an ever-growing proletariat."

This problem of abundance creating poverty is uniquely capitalist. In previous systems, people starved because not enough food had been created, but in capitalism, starvation can occur because too much food has been produced. In previous systems, homelessness resulted from a lack of housing, but in the aftermath of the 2008 financial crisis when "the housing bubble burst," many Americans lost their homes or became homeless because too much housing had been constructed.

Marxists often will cite a parable dialogue between a coal miner and his son.

Son: Father, I am very cold, why can't we light the stove?

Father: We cannot light the stove because we don't have any coal.

Son: Why don't we have any coal?

Father: Because I lost my job at the coal mine and we do not have any money to purchase coal.

Son: Why did you lose your job at the coal mine?

Father: Because there is too much coal.

Friedrich Engels explained why cyclical economic crises result from the built-in problem of production organized for profit in his text *Socialism: Utopian and Scientific,* writing: "The whole mechanism of the capitalist mode of production breaks down under the pressure of the productive forces, its own creations. It is no longer able to turn all this mass of means of production into capital. They lie fallow, and for that very reason the industrial reserve army must also lie fallow. Means of production, means of subsistence, available laborers, all the elements of production and of general wealth, are present in abundance."

Imperialism: The Capitalism of Our Time

Much of BreadTube's discussion of capitalism centers around the inequity of relations between employers and employees. This is certainly a very big aspect of Marxian analysis of capitalism. Marx described the alienating environment of the worker, the way workers are reduced to "appendages of machines" who sell their labor power to the employer like any other commodity. Marx described how the worker is not paid the full value of his labor, with the surplus value being stolen from in order to become the profits of the capitalist.

However, the bulk of Marx's analysis was focused on the problems that flow from production being organized for profits, as shown above. The irrational profit motive leads to capital centralizing into fewer and fewer hands, gluts overproduction, poverty amidst plenty, and all kinds of social chaos.

In the aftermath of Marx's death, Vladimir Lenin analyzed the further development of capitalism. Lenin showed that increasingly the industries became dominated by financial institutions, and that the banks who supply credit become the central institutions in western countries. In the 1890s, capitalism in the United States, Britain, France, Germany and other western countries became dominated by huge conglomerates. Banks and industries tied together in huge trusts as multinational corporations spread their tentacles across the globe. The western monopolies worked to stop economic development in Africa, Asia, and Latin America and maintain their dominance in global trade. Excess commodities were dumped onto the developing world that served as a captive market. This higher stage of capitalism was called "Imperialism."

Lenin described the five stages of imperialism: "We have to begin with as precise and full a definition of imperialism as possible. Imperialism is a specific historical stage of capitalism. Its specific character is threefold: imperialism is monopoly capitalism; parasitic, or decaying capitalism; moribund capitalism. The supplanting of free competition by monopoly is the fundamental economic feature, the quintessence of imperialism. Monopoly manifests itself in five principal forms: (1) cartels, syndicates and trusts—the concentration of production has reached a degree which gives rise to these monopolistic associations of capitalists; (2) the monopolistic position of the big banks—three, four or five giant banks manipulate the whole economic life of America, France, Germany; (3) seizure of the sources of raw material by the trusts and the financial oligarchy (finance capital is monopoly industrial capital merged with bank capital); (4) the (economic) partition of the world by the international cartels has begun. There are already over one hundred such international cartels, which command the entire world market and divide it "amicably" among themselves—until war redivides it. The export of capital, as distinct from the export of commodities under non-monopoly capitalism, is a highly characteristic phenomenon and is closely linked with the economic and territorial-political partition of the world; (5) the territorial partition of the world (colonies) is completed."

Vladimir Lenin composed his important book "Imperialism: The Highest Stage of Capitalism" in 1916, showing that capitalism had entered a stage of monopolistic domination of the world by banks and cartels based in western countries. The book reoriented Marxism to support national liberation struggles in the colonized world.

It is because of this global setup called imperialism that Nigeria can be the top oil producing country in Africa, exporting more of this valued commodity than any other country on the continent. Yet they still have only 62% literacy, along with a very low life expectancy and a high infant mortality rate, according to the *CIA World Factbook*.

It is because of imperialism that Honduras and Guatemala are drug and gang infested countries where much of the population lacks access to education and running water. In comparison, Nicaragua, which has broken out of imperialism, has been able to roll back poverty and raise living standards. The Central American countries that have economies and governments dominated by the United States are kept poor, subject to foreign domination and impoverishment.

When the British colonized India and Bangladesh, they burned the looms and forced people that had been weaving for thousands of years to import their cloth from British textile mills. In more recent times, the North American Free Trade Agreement (NAFTA) devastated the agricultural sectors of Mexico, Haiti, and other countries. Writing for the *New York Times* on November 24th, 2013, Laura Carlsen explained: "As heavily subsidized U.S. corn and other staples poured into Mexico, producer prices dropped and small farmers found themselves unable to make a living. Some two million have been forced to leave their farms since NAFTA. At the same time, consumer food prices rose, notably the cost of the omnipresent tortilla. As a result, 20 million Mexicans live in 'food poverty'. Twenty-five percent of the population does not have access to basic food and one-fifth of Mexican children suffer from malnutrition. Transnational industrial corridors in rural areas have contaminated rivers and sickened the population and typically, women bear the heaviest impact."

Much of the developing world is very rich in terms of natural resources and human labor. In order to maintain a monopoly, the western multinational corporations, with full support of the government apparatus and international institutions like the International Monetary Fund, the World Bank and the World Trade Organization, force countries into unnatural poverty due to foreign economic domination.

The mechanism for enforcing the rule of western monopolies is war. If countries break out of the grip of western capitalism and begin to develop their economies, they become subject to attack. If one looks at the economies of Russia, China, Venezuela, Iran, Cuba, Syria, or any other country the imperialists target for regime change, one will see a level of independence and striving toward development that the international monopolies cannot permit. Often this independence is directly related to the most valuable commodity in our outmoded fossil fuel economy, petroleum.

Vincent Copeland's text, *Expanding Empire,* describes in clear terms the nature of imperialist economics: "The expansion into foreign countries resulted from a new stage in the expansion of business: The export of capital. Business had been exporting ordinary commodities of trade for centuries. The export of capital was something new—especially for the United States. And it couldn't be done without foreign wars. The reason for this isn't very complicated. The export of capital goods—that is, machinery, mining equipment, railroad engines, earth-moving tools, etc., is intended not to make just a quick "small" profit, but a constantly repeating profit that can go on forever, if the exploiter can hold onto the "investment." The investment of capital in a foreign country should be regarded somewhat like sending a huge suction pump. The pump pulls out the metals from the ground, the products from the soil and the fruits from the trees—with the help, of course, of the labor of the "native" people working on this suction pump. It is as if the pump were connected to pipes that run back to the "home" country, via the banks and big corporations. All the rich products are showered from the pipes into the treasuries of these institutions, in the form of profits... Whole nations are drained by these great suction pumps—or "investments." And the profits are so great that rival groups of big business, led by small cliques of big banks, go to war with each other over the exploitation of these nations."

BreadTube voices tend to talk of capitalism in merely the simple factory floor analogies rather than understanding the concentration of global economic power in the hands of monopolistic associations. BreadTubers talk of "pencil factories" where workers produce the pencils, but a capitalist gets the profits. These analogies are certainly relevant in understanding the nature of capitalist production, but BreadTube voices obscure the big picture for a microcosm that obscures analysis of global events.

Furthermore, BreadTube voices tend to argue that anything resembling Lenin's analysis of capitalism in its imperialist stage is somehow anti-semitic. BreadTubers will often claim that references to bankers, international bankers, or globalism is merely a coded repackaging of Nazi conspiracy theories about Jewish global domination. This allegation is absurd, and would render not just all adherents of Marxism-Leninism, but also many liberal critics of globalization such as Noam Chomsky, Arundhati Roy, and Naomi Klein to be Nazi propagandists.

The world is not dominated by low level businessmen who own individual factories, but by an elite of ultra-rich, globally oriented capitalists. These capitalists do not focus their business efforts on a single national market. The ruling class of Wall Street and London are "globalists," and they dominate the world economy with gigantic financial institutions, "international banks." To analyze a world of gigantic multinational corporations that beat down entire nations simply in terms of the inequity between the owners of an allegorical pencil factory and his employees is simply inadequate. By declaring analysis of gigantic corporations or finance capitalists dominating the world to be "fascist" or "Trump-like" BreadTube is, in essence, blocking out and "cancelling" essential contemporary Marxist analysis.

Lenin's understanding of imperialism enabled him to reorient much of the Marxist movement. Marx argued that all nationalism was a barrier to workers solidarity, though in his later life he became somewhat sympathetic to the Irish freedom struggle. Marx argued that European colonialism was bringing development and progress to places like India. Lenin's understanding of how capitalism developed in the late 19th century laid the basis for revolutionaries embracing the national liberation struggles of colonized people. As the Chinese Communist Party's document *Long Live Leninism*, published April 16, 1960, summarizes: "Lenin pointed out that the oligarchy of finance capital in a small number of capitalist powers, that is, the imperialists, not only exploit the masses of people in their own countries, but oppress and plunder the whole world, turning most countries into their colonies and dependencies. Imperialist war is a continuation of imperialist politics."

Lenin understood that an aristocracy of labor, a strata of well paid workers enabled European social-democratic parties to become reformist and eventually support the First World War. Lenin saw that the revolutionary energy was coming from the east and the colonized world: "In the light of the law of the uneven economic and political development of capitalism, Lenin came to the conclusion that, because capitalism developed extremely unevenly in different countries, socialism would achieve victory first in one or several countries but could not achieve victory simultaneously in all countries."

Lenin argued that socialism in the developing world would come about with the working class leading the struggle to liberate entire nations from the yoke of imperialist domination. Because of the stratification of the working class within the imperialist homelands and the rise of social reformism and the aristocracy of labor, Communists in western countries had a special task: "The liberation movements of the proletariat in the capitalist countries should ally themselves with the national liberation movements in the colonies and dependent countries; this alliance can smash the alliance of the imperialists with the feudal and comprador reactionary forces in the colonies all dependent countries, and will therefore inevitably put a final end to the imperialist system throughout the world."

Imperialism, the rule of the world by western monopolies who keep the world poor in order to make themselves rich, is the capitalism of our time. Opposing capitalism in our time means opposing imperialism, and this understanding is essential, especially for those living in the imperialist world centers. The lack of any analysis of imperialism and anti-imperialism, and the constant allegation that those who do analyze such things are covert anti-semites reveals a very big flaw in the BreadTube sphere and its viewpoint.

The Marxist Definition of Socialism

Marxism views Socialism as resolving the inherent contradictions of capitalism, a system of production organized to make profits. Socialism is when the means of production become public property, and are forced by the state to serve society overall, not the profits of private owners. Marx distinguished between the "higher stage of Communism," the ultimate ideal of a stateless, classless world, and the lower stage of communism; i.e., socialism.

Marx, Engels, Lenin, and other scientific socialists specifically defined socialism, the lower stage of Communism. In the Communist Manifesto, Marx wrote: "The proletariat will use its political supremacy to wrest, by degree, all capital from the bourgeoisie, to centralize all instruments of production in the hands of the State; i.e., of the proletariat organized as the ruling class; and to increase the total productive forces as rapidly as possible. Of course, in the beginning, this cannot be effected except by means of despotic inroads on the rights of property, and on the conditions of bourgeois production; by means of measures, therefore, which appear economically insufficient and untenable, but which, in the course of the movement, outstrip themselves, necessitate further inroads upon the old social order, and are unavoidable as a means of entirely revolutionizing the mode of production. These measures will, of course, be different in different countries."

Marx went on to list in *The Communist Manifesto* 10 measures that the proletariat might adopt upon taking power in order to enact the transition to socialism. This list is commonly misrepresented by Libertarians and rightists, who point to planks such as "income tax" and "public education" as proof the USA is already a Communist country. Social-Democrats and reformists will also sometimes misrepresent this list.

In his pamphlet *Socialism: Utopian and Scientific*, Friedrich Engels also defined socialism. He wrote: "The proletariat seizes the public power, and by means of this transforms the socialized means of production, slipping from the hands of the bourgeoisie, into public property. By this act, the proletariat frees the means of production from the character of capital they have thus far borne, and gives their socialized character complete freedom to work itself out. Socialized production upon a predetermined plan becomes henceforth possible."

Using different words, Engels explained: "Whilst the capitalist mode of production more and more completely transforms the great majority of the population into proletarians, it creates the power which, under penalty of its own destruction, is forced to accomplish this revolution. Whilst it forces on more and more of the transformation of the vast means of production, already socialized, into State property, it shows itself the way to accomplishing this revolution. The proletariat seizes political power and turns the means of production into State property."

He also wrote: "This point is now reached. Their political and intellectual bankruptcy is scarcely any longer a secret to the bourgeoisie themselves. Their economic bankruptcy recurs regularly every 10 years. In every crisis, society is suffocated beneath the weight of its own productive forces and products, which it cannot use, and stands helpless, face-to-face with the absurd contradiction that the producers have nothing to consume, because consumers are wanting. The expansive force of the means of production bursts the bonds that the capitalist mode of production had imposed upon them. Their deliverance from these bonds is the one precondition for an unbroken, constantly-accelerated development of the productive forces, and therewith for a practically unlimited increase of production itself. Nor is this all. The socialized appropriation of the means of production does away, not only with the present artificial restrictions upon production, but also with the positive waste and devastation of productive forces and products that are at the present time the inevitable concomitants of production, and that reach their height in the crises. Further, it sets free for the community at large a mass of means of production and of products, by doing away with the senseless extravagance of the ruling classes of today, and their political representatives. The possibility of securing for every member of society, by means of socialized production, an existence not only fully sufficient materially, and becoming day-by-day more full, but an existence guaranteeing to all the free development and exercise of their physical and mental faculties — this possibility is now, for the first time, here, but it is here. With the seizing of the means of production by society, production of commodities is done away with, and, simultaneously, the mastery of the product over the producer. Anarchy in social production is replaced by systematic, definite organization. The struggle for individual existence disappears. Then, for the first time, man, in a certain sense, is finally marked off from the rest of the animal kingdom, and emerges from mere animal conditions of existence into really human ones."

In his book *The State and Revolution* Lenin defined socialism, the lower stage of Communism, in the following passages: "It is this communist society, which has just emerged into the light of day out of the womb of capitalism and which is in every respect stamped with the birthmarks of the old society, that Marx terms the "first", or lower, phase of communist society. The means of production are no longer the private property of individuals. The means of production belong to the whole of society. Every member of society, performing a certain part of the socially-necessary work, receives a certificate from society to the effect that he has done a certain amount of work. And with this certificate he receives from the public store of consumer goods a corresponding quantity of products. After a deduction is made of the amount of labor which goes to the public fund, every worker, therefore, receives from society as much as he has given to it."

Lenin also clarifies: "The first phase of communism, therefore, cannot yet provide justice and equality; differences, and unjust differences, in wealth will still persist." He then goes on to make clear: "And so, in the first phase of communist society (usually called socialism) "bourgeois law" is not abolished in its entirety, but only in part, only in proportion to the economic revolution so far attained; i.e., only in respect of the means of production. "Bourgeois law" recognizes them as the private property of individuals. Socialism converts them into common property. To that extent—and to that extent alone—"bourgeois law" disappears."

"Marx Wasn't A Statist"

Probably the most blatant distortion of Marxism that is spread in the BreadTube universe is the belief that somehow Marx did not believe in creating a centrally planned economy, or having the means of production become public property. As the previous quotations make clear, this is the very definitive act of the social revolution that overturns capitalism and creates socialism.

Yet, with smug arrogance and childish desperation, the BreadTube voices insist this cannot be the case. After all, they have been told by US media and educational institutions that each and every society where this transformation has taken place, it has resulted in a brutal human rights violating dictatorship and utter economic failure. Lacking the courage to question these narratives, like a Biblical creationist confronted by the fossil record, they seek to "reinterpret" Marx so both he and mainstream US media can be correct. They wish to uphold Marx, but discount and dismiss all who have put his ideas into practice in order to maintain respectability within (and funding from) the very institutions and society Marxism seeks to overturn.

Matt "Thought Slime" insists that Marx and Engels never called for a centrally planned economy. In a video released on February 5, 2021 entitled "Prager University Does Not Understand Democracy" the content creator simply bluffs, pretending that the quotations above do not exist and assuming that their audience will never bother to fact check assertions. Furthermore, Matt goes on to claim Lenin personally invented the idea of a centrally planned economy, calling his newly invented concept "Democratic Centralism."

A simple Google search for the term "Democratic Centralism" shows how laughingly inaccurate and ignorant this social-media appointed expert is. Democratic Centralism was the model for decision-making in Lenin's "party of new type." Democratic Centralism was a process through which the Bolshevik Party made decisions and obligated all members to carry them out. It distinguished the vanguard party model from the looser social-democratic organizing methods of the Russian Social-Democratic Labor Party; i.e., the Mensheviks. It has nothing to do with economic planning in a socialist state. It is a method of political organizing by Marxists under capitalism in order to take power. Such a gaffe should be embarrassing and discrediting, but Matt "Thought Slime" has not been discredited for spreading such blatant misinformation. Over 200,000 people have watched this mis-informative video about socialism, most of them probably believing its contents to be accurate.

Ian "Vaush" Kochinski, also speaking with the authority of the algorithms, frequently claims "Marx wasn't a statist." To justify this he utilizes a quotation from Marx's *Civil War in France*. Matt 'Thought Slime' also invokes this quotation, where Marx proclaims: "the working class cannot simply lay hold of the ready-made state machinery, and wield it for its own purposes."

The misuse of this quotation seethes with ignorance, if not blatant intentional deception. The passage comes from Marx's presentation *Civil War in France* in which he discusses the Paris Commune of 1871. This briefly existing regime that took power in Paris after the capitalist government had already surrendered to the Prussian invaders is considered by Marx to be the first historical example of his concept of "Dictatorship of the proletariat." Marx points to the Commune, not as an example of why states are not necessary, but rather for the lessons it taught about what post-capitalist states will look like.

The particular quote refers to the fact that the existing French state had been created to serve capitalism, and the Paris Communards who led the workers uprisings were forced to create *new* state institutions, not simply seize control of the previously existing ones created by capitalism. Marx spends the following paragraphs describing in detail the nature of the new proletarian forms of state power the Communards created and praising them. To claim this quote means Marx opposed states existing at all is laughable.

Here is the entire passage from Marx: "But the working class cannot simply lay hold of the ready-made state machinery, and wield it for its own purposes. The centralized state power, with its ubiquitous organs of standing army, police, bureaucracy, clergy, and judicature — organs wrought after the plan of a

Karl Marx pointed to the Paris Commune of 1871 as the first historical example of the Dictatorship of the Proletariat. His address "Civil War in France" describes in detail the new, working class government the communards created.

systematic and hierarchic division of labor — originates from the days of absolute monarchy, serving nascent middle class society as a mighty weapon in its struggle against feudalism. Still, its development remained clogged by all manner of medieval rubbish, seignorial rights, local privileges, municipal and guild monopolies, and provincial constitutions. The gigantic broom of the French Revolution of the 18th century swept away all these relics of bygone times, thus clearing simultaneously the social soil of its last hinderances to the superstructure of the modern state edifice raised under the First Empire, itself the offspring of the coalition wars of old semi-feudal Europe against modern France... The direct antithesis to the empire was the Commune. The cry of "social republic," with which the February Revolution was ushered in by the Paris proletariat, did but express a vague aspiration after a republic that was not only to supersede the monarchical form of class rule, but class rule itself. The Commune was the positive form of that republic... The first decree of the Commune, therefore, was the suppression of the standing army, and the substitution for it of the armed people. **The Commune was formed of the municipal councilors, chosen by universal suffrage in the various wards of the town, responsible and revocable at short terms. The majority of its members were naturally working men, or acknowledged representatives of the working class.**

The Commune was to be a working, not a parliamentary body, executive and legislative at the same time. Instead of continuing to be the agent of the Central Government, the police was at once stripped of its political attributes, and turned into the responsible, and at all times revocable, agent of the Commune... **Public functions ceased to be the private property of the tools of the Central Government. Not only municipal administration, but the whole initiative hitherto exercised by the state was laid into the hands of the Commune**... The judicial functionaries were to be divested of that sham independence which had but served to mask their abject subservience to all succeeding governments to which, in turn, they had taken, and broken, the oaths of allegiance... **The unity of the nation was not to be broken, but, on the contrary, to be organized by Communal Constitution, and to become a reality by the destruction of the state power which claimed to be the embodiment of that unity independent of, and superior to, the nation itself, from which it was but a parasitic excrescence."**

What Vaush claims about his cherry-picked quotation is nothing but blatant distortion. Either Kochinski was handed this quote by someone else and never bothered to look at the context, or he intentionally misrepresented its meaning with deceptive intent. To claim Marx was arguing that no central authority or state power should exist is simply inaccurate. On the contrary, Marx was emphasizing how new forms of state power must be created to correspond with the new class in power and its interests.

Maintaining Profits in Command

Armed with his misrepresentative quotes from Marx, Ian "Vaush" Kochinski has repeatedly said that socialism in the United States would mean "everything would be exactly the same except every corporation would be a worker cooperative." While worker ownership and cooperatives are not a bad thing, the problem with this definition of socialism is that it does not eliminate capitalism. Capitalism is a system where, as Engels put it, "the means of production only function as preliminary transformation into capital," or as Mao Zedong put it, "profits are in command." Simply instituting worker ownership does not eliminate what Marx called 'The Anarchy of Production.'

Employee stock ownership programs, co-determination, co-partnership, or profit sharing are not at all foreign to capitalism. Furthermore, those putting forth these ideas have generally not been socialists, but theoreticians and academics assigned with the task of making capitalist corporations more productive and efficient.

While BreadTube adherents fetishize the Mondragon

Corporation, a federation of worker cooperatives located in the Basque Region of Spain, the examples of such schemes within the capitalist system are much more widespread.

The Oxford University Act of 1854 in Britain required that the faculty of the University be represented on the board of directors. The Port of London Act of 1908 passed such a requirement for representation of dock workers on the board governing London's port. The Weimar Republic in Germany passed the Supervisory Board Act of 1922, requiring labor unions to have representation on the board of directors of corporations. Many western European countries maintain such laws up to today.

In the United States, the retirement plans offered to many corporate employees are described as "profit sharing plans" where the pension paid to retirees is related to the performance of the corporation. Many employees across the USA and the world have "stock options," incentive pay, and other mechanisms that theoretically make them co-owners of the corporation in which they work. Many different stock ownership, employee representation and co-ownership programs exist, and they vary in their degree of success.

During the 1920s and 30s, industrial unions often fought hard against "piece wages." Often factory employers would attempt to maximize their profits by paying employees only for each item produced, rather than a set hourly wage. In 1938, the Labor Movement celebrated the passage of the Fair Labor Standards Act which required all employees receive a minimum hourly wage on top of whatever incentives or productivity linked wages they received. These reforms

The passing of the Fair Labor Standards Act of 1938 was a key victory for the labor movement. It outlawed the paying of "piece wages" and required that all employees be given a minimum hourly wage.

brought a new level of economic security to industrial workers, because they knew how much money they would receive, rather than having their incomes subject to the unpredictable fluctuations of the market and however many products the capitalist assigned them to produce on a given workday.

BreadTube adherents will generally dismiss the many examples of their ideas being put into practice within capitalism. They will insist that piece wages, employee stock ownership programs, worker representation, co-partnership, and profit sharing are not enough. They will say they advocate 100% worker ownership and democratic control.

However, no matter how egalitarian and democratic a worker-cooperative model may be, it still does not eliminate the very essence of the capitalist system: profits in command. A worker-cooperative will seek to maximize profits for its employee shareholders.

Imagine if the US "defense industry" were operated under a worker-cooperative model. Would this end the "military industrial complex" long decried by leftists? Would the drive to make profits from war no longer influence US foreign policy? Not at all. If anything, the lust for war profits would expand beyond the corporate boardrooms to the factory floor. Employees would be motivated to see the government go to war and for government military spending to increase, as it would directly impact their incomes.

Having the guards as equal, democratic co-owners of private prisons would not eliminate the inherent societal problems flowing from the much decried "Prison Industrial Complex." Having workers as equal co-owners of pharmaceutical giants would not eliminate the drive to overprescribe potentially addictive or dangerous medications.

Other problems inherent to the capitalist system of production for profit would continue as well. Employee owners would certainly be incentivized to replace labor with machines, as the fewer workers hired by the cooperative firm, the larger their share of the profits would be. Employee owned enterprises would compete with other employee owned enterprises producing the same products and services. Environmental regulations and laws affecting other "externalities" would still be an impediment to the profits of corporate owners just as they are now, even if the corporate owners were the employees themselves. We could, of course, expect that "worker owners" would seek to lift regulations and maximize their own profits just as corporate owners would.

A system of "profits in command" is still irrational and unsustainable, even if those profits are shared. Simply declaring workers to be co-owners of profit centered entities functioning in the chaos of the market does not eliminate the irrationality of capitalism.

In the context of a state centrally planned economy,

worker-cooperative ownership is very different. The most successful examples of worker-cooperatives tend to be those that emerge in the absence of the anarchy of production, when an overall state central plan guides their activities.

The most successful example of a profit-sharing corporation, by far, is one that BreadTube avoids highlighting. The largest telecommunications manufacturer in the world is Huawei Technologies, a cooperative corporation established by the Chinese government and its military in 1988. An article in *Harvard Business Review* published on September 24, 2015 hails it as "A Case Study of When Profit Sharing Works" and speaks of the company in glowing terms. In the context of China's 5 year economic plans, receiving huge subsidies and directions from the state and military, Huawei has become very successful. The model of worker ownership, profit sharing, and coordination with state central planning and a socialist economy has made Huawei a model that many corporations in the capitalist world have studied. Huawei is widely respected for its efficiency and success. Of course, BreadTube voices largely remain silent on Huawei, as it takes the lead from the US State Department deeming anything associated with China or other anti-imperialist states to be toxic and evil.

Elements of "worker ownership" have been implemented in many socialist countries. The collectivization of agriculture in 1931 resulted in the prevalence of collective farms as the dominant form in the Soviet countryside. While some state farms that operated much like state owned factories existed, most of the Soviet Union's agriculture was carried out by independent kolkhozy, which sold agricultural goods to the state at a set rate. This motivated the farm workers to produce as much as possible in order to maximize the payout they would receive from the central government. This model became the dominant form of agriculture in "really existing socialism" of the Cold War, beyond the Soviet Union. Mao Zedong launched the creation of a collective farm system with his "Hail the Communes" campaign in the 1950s. Cuba, North Korea, and various Eastern European countries adopted the collective farm model. Trotsky criticized this, arguing that state farms were more socialistic in nature than collective farms and arguing that material incentives and differing abilities among farmers would lead to inequality. Stalin defended this model, arguing it was more efficient. Che Guevara and Mao Zedong both upheld the collective farm model as being more egalitarian and decentralized, and presented the Soviet Union as being a bit too centralized and bureaucratic in its planning of production, leading to a lack of participation by the working class and a level of alienation.

During the cultural revolution in China, the model of a "Three in One Combination" was adopted, where each factory was governed by an elected worker representative as well as a Communist Party official and a technical expert. Mao Zedong put forward the "Three in One Combination" as an alternative to the model of total factory autonomy put forward during the infamous "January Storm" of 1967, which established the Shanghai People's Commune.

Josip Broz Tito developed a model of "worker self-management." Albania declared this model to be state capitalism because it relied on material incentives to motivate labor, but other socialist countries considered Tito's model to be more effective. Tito's "worker self-management" model was most likely a big influence on Deng Xiaoping's "Reform and Opening Up" policies in 1978. Vietnam and Nicaragua have developed self-employment programs where workers become individual entrepreneurs in coordination with the state's overall vision. Venezuela has created many *colectivos* and communes, which produce goods and render services, while being subsidized with state revenue and directed by state central planners.

Worker-cooperatives are not bad, but the fetishization of them and the rejection of the need to eliminate the anarchy of production, distorts the nature of socialism. BreadTube's insistence that socialism is "everything exactly the same except every corporation is cooperative" is particularly problematic in the context of imperialism.

Capitalism in the 21st Century involves huge multinational corporations based in western countries reaping super profits at the expense of the developing world. Wars are waged to enforce that system, with socialist and anti-imperialist governments being the primary targets. Imperialism is a global economic order in which the world is made poor and kept poor, so that the finance capitalists of London and Wall Street can remain rich.

Simply offering a greater share of the super profits of empire to the workers within the imperialist homeland is not dismantling this global system. If anything, it is a scheme that would likely stabilize and enhance it.

The Myth of the 20th Century

Underlying BreadTube's redefinition of socialism is the same motivation and sentiments that are highly present in Trotskyism, Anarchism, Social-Democracy and other brands of left-wing anti-communism. In the United States, anti-communist propaganda about the 20th Century is widespread and inculcated among the population. It is so central to the rhetoric of every faction of the ruling class that repeating it is almost mandatory for any voice that seeks to avoid being marginalized.

In order to conform to the 'party line' that is almost universal among every faction of the US ruling class, BreadTube must accept the premise that "Communism failed everywhere it has ever been tried."

It is tragic that so many adherents of socialism, who claim to oppose the capitalist system, are so cowardly that they cannot state what is obvious, socialism works. When Yale economist Dr. Richard Wolff debated Steven "Destiny" Bonnell, he confronted this mythology head on, proclaiming: "I have no idea what this silly remark that I so often hear that no socialist society has succeeded at anything, I have no idea what you are talking about. Let me give you an example, one of the most important metrics used in the economics profession around the world to assess the success of an economic system is the rate of economic growth. You measure GDP and you look at how it grows over time, and then you compare one country to another to assess their relative success, not as societies, because that's a vague generality... It's not the only metric, but it's a widely used one so I am now going to use it. In the 20th century the fastest growing GDP in any country measured was the Soviet Union. And in the 21st century we are living in, the fastest growing GDP in the world has been the People's Republic of China. This is not an endorsement of one or another economic system, it's a statement of fact verified by any reliable source of information, the UN, the projects of the

University of California at Berkeley and others who keep track of this."

Bonnell quibbled, trying to say that Japan had been more successful than the Soviet Union and that the industrialization of the USSR was irrelevant because many countries underwent similar growth at the time. Wolff further ripped this illogic to shreds proclaiming: "Those are the facts, you can play whatever games you want, the fact of the matter is that the Soviet Union's performance in the 20th century completely outshines that of Japan. In 1917 when the Soviet Union began, it was the poorest country in Europe by far. It then goes through 70 years of World War 1, of a civil war, of collectivization, and of World War 2, which did more damage in Russia than in any other country. Notwithstanding that it was the poorest country at the beginning of this horrific story, it ends up in 1965 being the number one competitor of the United States for global hegemony. That's only because of its number one status in economic growth that it achieved the overcoming of all those horrific losses. I am not arguing in favor of this or that about the Soviet Union, but the fact of its achievement is a staggering reality that you can dance around today and tomorrow, but it doesn't go away because it is inconvenient to confront it. The same thing is true now. If you read Pearl Buck's novels about China before the revolution, you will read about a society whose depth of poverty literally blows your mind, and here they are about to surpass the United States by the end of this decade, and that was accomplished by a Communist revolution and a government that has been run by a Communist Party to this day."

BreadTube's insistence that socialism is merely a worker cooperative scheme reveals further the thesis of this book, that BreadTube is largely the creation of the more powerful, globalist wing of the ruling class in its efforts to beat back the rebellions of Trump and lower level capitalists. The pro-imperialist narrative, where Communist revolutions "only made life worse" is repeated by BreadTube voices, despite being overwhelmingly inconsistent with reality. Because BreadTube targets the same governments that the US State Department targets, and repeats the same narrative of the 20th Century that is widely promoted in US society, it also allows the most common argument against socialism to go unchallenged.

Right-wingers have long mocked the comment, "That's not real socialism," which BreadTube aligned voices frequently fall back on. During the Iraq War, right-wingers who taunted leftists would carry sarcastic placards reading "Communism only killed 200 million people, let's try it again!" There is a refusal of leftists to challenge the historical record; not about human rights or the shortcomings of existing socialist societies, but about basic economic data. This is the greatest weakness of the socialist movement in the United States. However, it fits with the overall weakness of BreadTube's analysis, which is a refusal to confront or discuss imperialism, in an age where western capitalism IS imperialism.

Basic economic data shows that the Soviet Union had a consistently high rate of economic growth throughout its existence. In 1917, Russia was an agrarian underdeveloped country. By 1936 the Soviet Union was fully electrified and had become an industrial powerhouse. The Soviet Union produced more steel and tractors than any other country in the world. It wiped out illiteracy, built a modern university system, and constructed some of the largest power plants in the world. In the field of culture, the Soviet Union spawned the films of Sergei Eisenstein, the music of Shostakovich, and some of the greatest ballet performers and Olympic athletes.

With an economy where the state controls the major industries and banks and issues 5 year economic plans, China has become the second largest economy on earth, lifting 800 million people from poverty. Cuba's achievements in terms of healthcare and literacy are marveled at by international observers. Prior to the fall of the Soviet Union, North Korea experienced huge explosions of growth with Soviet aid. A BBC article from August 26, 2008 admits: "The mass mobilization of the population, along with Soviet and Chinese technical assistance and financial aid, resulted in annual economic growth rates estimated to have reached 20%, even 30%, in the years following the devastating 1950-53 Korean war. As late as the 1970s, South Korea languished in the shadow of the "economic miracle" north of the border."

Baathist Arab Socialism in Iraq and Syria resulted in massive economic achievements in terms of literacy, education, and industrialization. Years of pro-western regimes have not undone the great achievements of Gamal Abdel Nasser, who took great strides to industrialize Egypt, constructing the Aswan Dam in coordination with the Soviet Union. Kwame Nkrumah, Julius Nyerere, Muammar Gaddafi, and other African revolutionaries who established socialist planned economies achieved similar victories in terms of basic societal health. The Islamic System labelled "Not Capitalism But Islam," in which the state and the Revolutionary Guards control the commanding heights of economic power has resulted in a huge level of development in Iran.

Criticisms of these societies related to issues like human rights, consumer goods, or other issues are certainly reasonable. To say Marxist-Leninist governments and anti-imperialist states "never accomplished anything" or "only made life worse" is a sick joke that is completely contrary to all basic economic data.

However, BreadTube's vision of socialism as merely profit centered worker cooperatives, its demonization of the very same governments the imperialists target, all make BreadTube a version of socialism that is deemed acceptable by the ruling class. In rare instances BreadTubers will even defend cuts in social spending and the erosion of the welfare state, arguing that "we don't want state socialism" and "socialism has nothing to do with the government." Somehow various adherents of BreadTube thinking have determined neoliberal economics and austerity is not a threat to socialism, because their worker cooperative schemes will still be permitted.

It is clear that BreadTube has created a brand of "socialism" that is not very threatening to the status quo. Rather than calling for society to control the means of production, even a minimal class struggle program like stopping cuts in social spending or opposing imperialist regime change wars, BreadTube simply wants to experiment with profit sharing and employee stock ownership as imperialism and austerity are allowed to roll ahead.

Not surprisingly, this deviation from everything Marxists and socialists have advocated for hundreds of years has been enabled to go viral and speak in the place of genuine anti-capitalism.

Chapter Three: Nazi! Nazi! Nazi!

Biden's first joint address to Congress, delivered on April 28, 2021 contained some subtle but dangerous rhetoric. In his opening, Biden invoked the January 6th Capitol Riot when Trump supporters vandalized the halls of US Congress: "As I stand here tonight — just one day shy of the 100th day of my administration. 100 days since I took the oath of office, lifted my hand off our family Bible, and inherited a nation in crisis. The worst pandemic in a century. The worst economic crisis since the Great Depression. The worst attack on our democracy since the Civil War."

Biden used the bulk of his address to promise sweeping economic reforms such as infrastructure, healthcare, guaranteed college and labor union protections. The speech was far more social-democratic in its content than anything heard from a US President in recent decades. However, underlying the progressive economic content was hostility to a number of countries, most especially the People's Republic of China.

"We're in a competition with China and other countries to win the 21st Century. We have to do more than just build back. We have to build back better," he told the American people: "In my discussion with President Xi, I told him that we welcome the competition — and that we are not looking for conflict... No responsible American president can remain silent when basic human rights are violated. A president has to represent the essence of our country. America is an idea — unique in the world." Throughout the speech Biden used the word "autocrat" to refer to anti-imperialist governments.

In the final moments of the speech, Biden spelled things out more clearly: "America's adversaries — the autocrats of the world — are betting it can't. They believe we are too full of anger and division and rage. They look at the images of the mob that assaulted this Capitol as proof that the sun is setting on American democracy. They are wrong... We have stared into an abyss of insurrection and autocracy — of pandemic and pain — and "We the People" did not flinch."

"Insurrection and Autocracy"

Biden's use of phrase "insurrection and autocracy" after referring to anti-imperialist leaders as "autocrats" was an attempt to equate the right-wing crowds that participated in the January 6th events with the governments of Russia, China, Iran, Venezuela, Cuba, and North Korea.

However, this is simply the opposite of reality. The bulk of Trump's crowd of supporters chanting "Stop The Steal" were white Americans of working class or middle class origin. However, a big chunk of the crowd were from specific right-wing immigrant constituencies long cultivated by the US intelligence apparatus to fight against anti-imperialist countries.

The Falun Gong religious cult that opposes the Chinese Communist Party and publishes the *Epoch*

At the January 6th pro-Trump demonstration that escalated to the infamous Capitol Riot, many adherents of the anti-communist Falun Gong religious cult were present. Anti-Communist Cubans, Koreans and Venezuelans were also well represented. BreadTube's attempt to paint the Capitol Riot as somehow linked to anti-imperialist countries is completely dishonest.

Times were among the protesters. This group of anti-communists glorify feudalism in China and call the empowerment of women since 1949 a sign that the world is in a "Dharma Ending Period." The group is very hostile to LGBT people. Supporters of the anti-communist riots in Hong Kong were also present.

Supporters of the Pahlavi Monarchy, deposed by Iran's 1979 Islamic Revolution, were present, unfurling the monarchist flag and chanting against the Islamic Republic.

Busloads of Cuban anti-Communists from Miami, along with exiled rich from Venezuela, Nicaragua, and Bolivia, were at the rally echoing Rudy Giuliani's claim that the US elections had been rigged by Communists.

A large number of Israeli flags were unfurled as supporters of Netanyahu and the Likud Party marched in support of the man who murdered Qassem Soleimani and moved the US embassy to Jerusalem.

Joe Biden's attempt to link the Capitol Riot with the progressive anti-imperialist states targeted by US imperialism was simply inaccurate. This was a pro-imperialist mob. The Proud Boys chanted "west is the best" and the forces blamed for the supposed rigging of the vote were Chinese Communists and Bolivarian Socialists. To think this right-wing crowd of anti-communists, Zionists, feudalists, libertarians, and anti-Islamic bigots have anything in common with the emerging block of 21st Century Socialism around the world is an absurd delusion. However, this distortion fits the narrative of mainstream US media and BreadTube.

Endless attention was given to the racist Confederate Flag displayed by white nationalists and neo-confederates who attended the rally, while the various highly visible pro-imperialist counter-gangs were ignored. The narrative of mainstream US media echoed by BreadTube is that the bulk of America's working class are racist white trash and that Donald Trump was a Nazi attempting to stir them up. This suggests that this "populism" somehow is the equivalent of Bolivarian Socialism, Chinese Communism, or the Islamic Revolution of Iran.

The Proud Boys, a racist organization that participated in the January 6th Capitol Riot, chants "West is the Best" at their gatherings. This belief that western capitalist countries are superior to anti-imperialist and socialist countries is shared by most BreadTube commentators.

The enemy in the BreadTube narrative is "Populism" and socialist governments around the world are just another variant of this evil, the equivalent of fascism. When the ignorant, inferior working people are rising up and demanding that the state protect them, rallying around a charismatic leader, this is a threat to the non-conformity and freedom of the superior caste of cosmopolitan intellectuals.

This bizarre narrative that views average Americans as the enemy and equates socialist states that control the means of production with Nazi gas chambers, has nothing to do with Marxism. However, it is not new. It is a narrative that was carefully cultivated by the Congress for Cultural Freedom and covert manipulation of intellectual discourse throughout the Cold War. BreadTube has taken this toxic narrative to a new, far more illogical and far more absurd level, in an attempt to defend the liberal order from right-wing opposition.

"A counter-revolutionary mass movement"

Among Marxists and scientific socialists, three narrative definitions of fascism are commonly used.

The most common narrative, repeated by social-democrats and mainline Communist parties, is that fascism is merely a right-wing dictatorship. If conservatives become more authoritarian and totalitarian this represents "creeping fascism." This is the narrative usually used by leftists in the United States to justify voting for the Democratic Party, as Republicans are presented as potential Hitlers.

The second definition, put forward by Trotskyites, is that fascism is an ever present middle class political movement that condemns both big capital and the labor movement. Trotskyites argue that the current is utilized by big capital to wage a campaign of violence against socialist revolutionaries and progressives in times of capitalist crisis in order to lay the basis for a police and military state.

The third definition of fascism, utilized by the Soviet aligned parties during the "Third Period" of 1928-1935 following the Sixth Congress of the Communist International, is that fascism is a cheap capitalist imitation of socialism used to prevent revolution and stabilize the economy in a crisis. On this basis, the Comintern referred to social democrats, who at the time called for the political repression of Communists, as 'social fascists.'

All of these definitions contain an element of truth, but all of them miss the essence of fascism. Fascism is defined by a mass mobilization of destruction and driving down of living conditions intended to resolve an economic crisis.

As Georgi Dimitrov, the leader of the Communist International explained in 1935: "With the development of the very deep economic crisis, with the general crisis of capitalism becoming sharply accentuated and the mass of working people becoming revolutionized, fascism has embarked upon a wide offensive. The ruling bourgeoisie more and more seeks salvation in fascism, with the object of taking exceptional predatory measures against the working people, preparing for an imperialist war of plunder, attacking the Soviet Union, enslaving and partitioning China, and by all these means preventing revolution.

Fascism involves a mobilization of society to destroy and drive down living standards in the hopes of resolving an economic crisis.

The imperialist circles are trying to shift the whole burden of the crisis onto the shoulders of the working people. That is why they need fascism. They are trying to solve the problem of markets by enslaving the weak nations, by intensifying colonial oppression and repartitioning the world anew by means of war. That is why they need fascism. They are striving to forestall the growth of the forces of revolution by smashing the revolutionary movement of the workers and peasants and by undertaking a military attack against the Soviet Union — the bulwark of the world proletariat. That is why they need fascism."

The most scientific study of fascism is *Fascism and Social Revolution*, written by British Communist intellectual R. Palme Dutt in 1934 after Hitler took power in Germany. Dutt explained what fascism is in practice: "to endeavor to strangle the powers of production, to arrest development, to destroy material and human forces, to fetter international exchange, to check science and invention, to crush the development of ideas and thought, and to concentrate on the organization of limited, self-sufficient, non-progressive hierarchic societies in a state of mutual war-in short, to force back society to a more primitive stage in order to maintain the existing class domination. This is the path of Fascism, the path to which the bourgeoisie in all modern countries where it rules is increasingly turning, the path of human decay."

Dutt rips to shreds the notion that there is some set of ideas or principles that define fascism as a distinct political ideology or economic system. Dutt writes: "Fascism in this specific or narrower sense is marked by definite familiar characteristics: in the case of the Fascist movements, by the characteristics of terrorism, extralegal fighting formations, anti-parliamentarism, national and social demagogy, etc.; in the case of the completed Fascist dictatorships, by the suppression of all other parties and organisations, and in particular the violent suppression of all independent working-class organisation, the reign of terror, the 'totalitarian' state, etc."

After summarizing the diverse creeds, principles, economic theories, mythologies, and rhetorical styles utilized by fascists, Dutt shows that all of them are mere bombast. Fascism is defined by action in the form of political violence and repression, not any clear set of principles: "All these abstract general conceptions which are paraded as the peculiar outlook of Fascism have no distinctive character whatever, but are common to a thousand schools of bourgeois political philosophy, which are not yet Fascist, and in particular to all national-conservative schools... Fascism, in fact, developed as a movement in practice, in the conditions of threatening proletarian revolution, as a counter-revolutionary mass movement supported by the bourgeoisie, employing weapons of mixed social demagogy and terrorism to defeat the revolution and build up a strengthened capitalist state dictatorship; and only later endeavored to adorn and rationalise this process with a 'theory.' It is in this actual historical

British Communist theoretician R. Palme Dutt composed the important book "Fascism and Social Revolution" in 1934, giving the most in-depth and scientific understanding of fascism in this era.

process that the reality of Fascism must be found, and not in the secondary derivative attempts post festum at adornment with a theory."

Dutt points out that unlike revolutionary leftist movements, Fascism does not achieve power through struggle, but rather, is called upon by the power structure after a long period of grooming: "Fascism has never 'conquered power' in any country. In every case Fascism has been placed in power from above by the bourgeois dictatorship. In Italy Fascism was placed in power by the King, who refused to sign the decree of martial law against it, and invited Mussolini to power; Mussolini's legendary 'March on Rome' took place in a Wagon-Lit sleeping-car. In Germany Fascism was placed in power by the President, at a time when it was heavily sinking in support in the country, as shown by the elections. The bourgeoisie, in fact, has in practice passed power from one hand to the other, and called it a 'revolution,' while the only reality has been the intensified oppression of the working class. After the establishment of the full Fascist dictatorship, the policy has been still more openly and completely, despite a show of a few gestures of assistance to small capital, the most unlimited and ruthless policy of monopolist capital. The whole machinery of Fascism mercilessly turned against those of its former supporters who have been innocent enough to expect some anti-capitalist action and called for a 'second revolution.'"

The Myth of Fascist Ideology and Aesthetics

This scientific understanding of fascism as an attempt to stabilize capitalist society amid a crisis through brute force, economic regression, and a mobilization of destruction and barbarism leading toward war was the understanding used by those who were most successful in defeating fascism. The Communists who mobilized to beat back Oswald Mosley in Britain at the 1936 Battle of Cable Street held this understanding of fascism. The underground resistance in Germany and the occupied countries which sabotaged armaments and bombed railways was led by Communists who had this understanding of fascism. The Red Army that liberated Auschwitz concentration camp and eventually took Berlin had this understanding of fascism.

However, since the end of the Second World War, there has been a huge attempt to erode this scientific understanding and replace it with one that is more convenient for the western capitalists. Recognizing that fascism emerges from the natural workings and failures of capitalism is certainly an argument in favor of socialism and against the capitalist system. Undermining this definition and replacing it with subjective, aesthetic, and philosophical obfuscations has been a key task of the US intelligence apparatus.

The Congress for Cultural Freedom formed in 1949 as an association of left-wing artists, scientists, and academics who opposed Communism is considered by the US Central Intelligence Agency to be one of its most successful operations. The organization was funded by the CIA and the Trotskyite Irving Kristol, an associate of Max Shachtman, who later became known as the "Father of Neoconservatism," was selected to lead the operation. Literary magazines such as *Partisan Review, Encounter, Paris Review* and *Der Monat* were subsidized and circulated throughout the United States, Britain, and western countries to nudge leftist circles away from the Soviet perspective.

Theodor Adorno, a Marxist intellectual associated with the Frankfurt School, had his work subsidized and promoted as part of the Congress for Cultural Freedom operation. His work was published in *Der Monat*, and his research for *The Authoritarian Personality* was conducted with individuals tied to the Tavistock Institute of Human Relations, an entity widely known to be utilized for research by British intelligence.

The conclusions of Adorno's writing on the concept of an "Authoritarian Personality" are a complete departure from scientific Marxism.

Among his sources, Adorno cites the crackpot psychoanalyst Wilhelm Reich, infamous for his "orgone machine" that supposedly captured a magical energy source created from human orgasms. Reich also claimed that he was in contact with extraterrestrial creatures. Much like the crackpot Reich who was expelled from Psychoanalysis by Freud and expelled from the German Communist Party before moving to

Psychoanalyst Wilhelm Reich was convicted of fraud by the Food and Drug Administration, for marketing an "Orgone Machine" that had no real medical value. Reich's narrative that Nazism is rooted in sexual repression is a key influence on Theodor Adorno, Susan Sontag and the Synthetic Left's reinterpretation of fascism.

New York City in the 1930s, Adorno argues that fascism is rooted in psychological and cultural trends, not the breakdown of capitalism.

Among the various leftist intellectuals and cultural critics who are now documented to have been covertly promoted by the US intelligence in the post-WW2 years, a new narrative exists about what fascism is. Adorno documents an "authoritarian personality" of individuals who are deemed to be deviant because they would be predisposed to be part of a mass political movement, and seek to make sacrifices for causes greater than themselves.

Susan Sontag, another CIA favorite, spent pages reflecting on the "fascist aesthetic" in a *New York Times Review of Books* piece. In Sontag's mind fascism is "extravagant effort, and the endurance of pain... the massing of groups of people; the turning of people into things; the multiplication and replication of things and grouping of people/things around an all-powerful hypnotic leader-figure or force. The fascist dramaturgy centers on the orgiastic transactions between mighty forces and their puppets, uniformly garbed and shown in swelling numbers. Its choreography alternates between ceaseless motions and a congealed, static, "virile" posing... "mass athletic demonstration, a choreographed display of bodies are a valued activity in all totalitarian countries; and the art of the gymnast, so popular now in Eastern Europe, also evokes recurrent features of fascist aesthetics; the holding in or confining of force; military precision."

Hannah Arendt, a favorite of the *Partisan Review* milieu, composed a book entitled *Eichmann in Jerusalem*, which was widely praised. In the book she put forward the widely celebrated concept of the "banality of evil" arguing that genocidal Nazi war criminal Adolph Eichmann was just an ordinary person, essentially making the case that all populism and mass mobilizations are fascistic in essence, because deep down ordinary working class people are potential Nazis.

All of these concepts and redefinitions were implied throughout the cultural revolution of the 1960s and 70s, when long haired counterculture youth decried their pro-military right-wing parents as "fascists." This redefinition of fascism to be "people working together in groups for a common aim" or "people acting like responsible adults and controlling their impulses" flowed from the *New York Times*, academia, and everywhere else in US society.

The ultimate purpose of this non-materialist, idealist retelling of the 1930s was revealed in 1982, when Susan Sontag spilled the beans in front of a crowd of protesters who had gathered to protest in support of the anti-communist and anti-semitic Solidarsnoc dock workers of Poland. Sontag said: "Communism is Fascism—successful Fascism, if you will. What we have called Fascism is, rather, the form of tyranny that can be overthrown—that has, largely, failed. I repeat: not only is Fascism (and overt military rule) the probable destiny of all Communist societies—especially when their populations are moved to revolt—but Communism is in itself a variant, the most successful variant, of Fascism. Fascism with a human face."

Susan Sontag equated the Red Army that took Berlin, the Abraham Lincoln Brigade volunteers who fought Franco in Spain, the activists who organized in support for the Scottsboro Nine against Jim Crow, and almost all of the greatest heroes of the 1930s and 40s, with the very entity they successfully defeated.

To the Synthetic Left, brought to you by the CIA, fascism is not a form of Bonapartism intended to hold off revolution as capitalism enters a crisis. Rather, it is people refusing to become atomized and easily controlled individuals, and holding on to any notion of solidarity and joint effort. Progressives who refuse to embrace their individualist anti-populism that view average working people as a dangerous mob, most especially Communists, are deemed to be fascists.

Natalie Wynn's "F@scists"

Natalie "Contrapoints" Wynn, the shining star of the BreadTube internet sphere, who stands shoulders above her colleagues in terms of production values and coherent narrative, gained mainstream appreciation for her video "Decrypting the Alt-Right: How to Recognize a F@scist."

While much of Contrapoints work contains useful insights, this particular video is almost comedic at points. One is forced to think of the 1964 film *Dr. Strangelove* which mocked the anti-communist hysteria. In the film a particularly crazed general speaks obsessively about "bodily fluids" and brags that he only drinks rainwater because he believes most liquids have been contaminated by a secret communist conspiracy.

Contrapoints begins the video stating "contemporary fascists hold three core beliefs." She lists them as a belief in the sacredness of the white race, the conspiracy theory that Jews seek to conduct "white genocide" or "replacement," and the ultimate goal of creating a "white ethno-state" in which non-whites and "degenerates" are "purged."

This is certainly an accurate description of what white nationalists believe. However, the right-wing, especially in the age of the internet, is far more vast and ideologically diverse. Many far-rightists are Anarcho-Capitalists who advocate unregulated free market capitalism. They want no government intervention whatsoever in the economy or on matters of sex, race, or social justice. Many far-rightists are anti-Islamic bigots who do not believe Jews are a secret cabal, but rather see Israel an outpost of civilization against the menace of Islam. Far right circles are full of followers of Julius Evola, traditionalist Catholics, Neo-Confederates, Libertarians, Incels, etc. The white national current exists as one of many strands of dissident right wing thought.

Contrapoints then spends the rest of the video developing all kinds of loopholes through which individuals who have nothing in common with white nationalism can be linked to it: "So if you want to recognize a fascist, you have to know how to read subtext and hear dog whistles because 99 times out of a hundred, a fascist will disavow fascism, racism, and white supremacy, at least when talking to you, a non-fascist," Contrapoints explains, "I am not a fascist is exactly what a fascist would say."

Is it true that many White Nationalists conceal their views, and operate covertly in broader conservative circles? Yes. It is true that many advocates of a white ethnostate who harbor anti-semitic views will conceal this message when creating broader content? Yes.

However, Contrapoints video basically argues that anything can be a dog whistle, anyone can be a fascist, and all that is necessary to prove it is something as meaningless as a hand gesture, a slip of the tongue, or most importantly a disagreement with the mainstream of the left.

The overwhelming majority of people in the United States feel patriotic, but according to Contrapoints, statements like "I love my country" could be interpreted as coded fascist messaging. Gestures like "Thumbs up" or "OK" signs are used by millions of Americans each day, but according to Contrapoints, these could indeed be secret Nazi hand signs.

Contrapoints video would be laughable if it were not taken seriously by many of the millions of people who viewed it. One of the primary targets of this bizarre cancel culture conspiracy theory is anti-imperialist leftists. Across the internet, commentators like Jimmy Dore, Kim Iverson, and others who do not agree with US foreign policy are considered to be "fascists" and "crypto-fascists."

The proof is that they support anti-imperialist countries like China, Syria, Venezuela, Russia, etc. These countries have been declared "fascist" by US media, and therefore anyone who shows sympathy with them is "fascist" by default.

If you are reminded of McCarthyism, you should be. If one showed sympathy for the Soviet Union or Mao's China during the 1950s, you were dismissed as "a communist." Careers and lives were destroyed by the House Un-American Activities Committee. Organizations with the word "worker" in their name were falsely accused of being Communist front groups. Individuals were forced to disavow their friends, relatives, and co-workers.

McCarthyism was a mobilization to silence all critics

of US foreign policy as the Cold War exploded following the Second World War. In the New Cold War, BreadTube is being utilized to destroy the lives and careers of all who don't echo the rhetoric against Russia and China.

Contrapoints and BreadTube do not apply this "guilt by association" and conspiratorial decoding to liberals. Joe Biden can salute the flag, shake hands with Republicans, give a thumbs up, or do whatever he wants and not be declared "fascist" by BreadTube. Joe Biden's series of racial gaffes, his string of sexual assaults, rape allegations from Tara Reade, his support for the Iraq war, his crime bills, are all forgivable mistakes. None of these vicious actions and blatantly racist words render Joe Biden to be part of the secret fascist conspiracy that sits at the center of the BreadTube worldview. Why? Unlike the right-wing and the legitimate anti-imperialist left, he defends the status quo, so by definition he cannot be fascist.

BreadTube routinely insists phrases like "International Bankers" or "Western Civilization" are fascist dog whistles, yet Hillary Clinton's use of the term "superpredators" is deemed to be merely an understandable mistake or error. Legitimate anti-imperialists are routinely baited for supporting anti-imperialist states like Russia or China, deemed "fascist" by mainstream media. However, the Democratic Party's embracing of Israel, Saudi Arabia, and other US aligned regimes that violate human rights never renders them "Red Browns" or "Crypto-Fascists."

Contrapoints video has been utilized to destroy the lives of countless individuals. Internet harassment campaigns are mobilized frequently against all kinds of people. Jeopardy contestants, adolescents on social media, confused conservatives, random Trump supporters, legitimate anti-imperialist leftists, and all who do not immediately bow before NATO and the Pentagon run the risk of being declared a "literal Nazi" by the internet cult of "anti-fascists" who demand 100% adherence to MSNBC talking points.

Like much of BreadTube, Contrapoints ideology is inconsistent. Sometimes she seems like a social-democrat or anarchist, but other times it seems like she is merely a pro-establishment warrior working to purge the US government apparatus of an evil "secret fascist conspiracy" that has taken it over. Much like the anti-semitic narrative that views western capitalism and imperialism as inherently good, but merely corrupted by a sinister cabal, Contrapoints seems to argue that the evils of American capitalism are due to a sinister conspiracy of white nationalists, not the system itself. If only this conspiracy can be purged, everything will be fine.

Of course, in the world view extolled by much of BreadTube, if you dare disagree that the west is a bastion of tolerance and freedom, while China, Russia, Syria, and Venezuela are evil "fascist" regimes, you must be a fascist yourself. Who cares if you are anti-racist, or have spent over a decade working against racism; remember: "I am not a fascist is exactly what a fascist would say."

The cancel culture conspiracy belief in which almost every conservative and every dissident leftist is part of a secret white nationalist cabal that must be stopped at all costs is not an honest delusion. Much like the John Birch Society of the early 1960s, the conspiracy theory has been weaponized to serve one wing of the political establishment in its fight against the other. The intent is to cultivate a mob of paranoid fanatics who will function as the foot soldiers of the establishment.

A Gift to Actual Fascism

Hilariously, according to Contrapoints, she herself must be a fascist. Throughout her video she wears a Nazi-esque costume, shows images highlighting the work of far-right commentators (despite disavowing them, something she claims doesn't matter), and shows various hand signs and images known to be coded fascist imagery.

Furthermore, it is worth noting that claiming innocuous gestures and symbols are "fascist" was actually a stated maneuver of white nationalists at one point. The idea was to make the left look delusional, paranoid and stupid by claiming all kinds of benign things were "fascist." It appears this maneuver has been effective.

Though the BreadTube community and its content is certainly loved by the YouTube algorithms, few Americans have been convinced that most of their friends and neighbors who use the wrong words or question US foreign policy are part of a secret white nationalist cabal. Right-wing figures like Jordan Peterson have certainly benefited from popular disgust at cancel culture. Much like many Cold War Republicans, Contrapoints lives in an alternate universe where the world consists of two types of people: those who agree with her and the US status quo, and those who are part of a vast conspiracy of people pretending to believe all sorts of different things, but in reality they are all working for the same sinister agenda. It is a vast conspiracy against our American way of life. Watch out for your precious bodily fluids!

This kind of childish black-and-white totalitarian thinking is what much of the Cold War Synthetic Left was intended to undermine. The Congress for Cultural Freedom and the Frankfurt school were funded in order to undermine the dichotomy of "with us or against us" that often led to marginalized people like African-Americans or LGBT people becoming sympathetic to the Soviet Union. Now, hilariously, the very mindset the Synthetic Left was set up to combat is being promoted by it: Agree with them (and US foreign policy) or no matter what you say or really believe, you are working for the fascists.

The entire reason the Synthetic Left was covertly funded by the CIA is due to the reality that the Communist Party USA and the various Marxist-Leninists of the world were on the vanguard of combating racism and fascism. The Soviet Union brought the petition of William L. Patterson entitled *We Charge Genocide* to the United Nations, exposing the horrific realities facing Black Americans. The Soviet

BreadTube commentators regularly equate Communists with white supremacists and Neo-Nazis despite the historical legacy of the two political currents being completely opposite. Pro-Soviet Communists such as William L. Patterson, Nelson Peery, Paul Robeson and Harry Haywood were key in building the Civil Rights Congress and opposing Jim Crow segregation.

Union convened demonstrations in the 1930s in support of the Scottsboro Nine, a group of African American men falsely accused of rape. Paul Robeson, Henry Winston, James W. Ford, Langston Hughes and many of the most anti-racist and anti-fascist voices in US society were sympathetic to or even joined the Communist Party USA. The Communist Party formed the Civil Rights Congress to fight for African-Americans in the southern USA.

While the US government coddled and did business with Hitler, Communists rallied against him from day one. In 1935, Communist Party USA members led by Bill Bailey attacked a Nazi ship that had docked in the New York harbor, and ripped down the swastika flag. While the US government did nothing to aid the Spanish Republic, members of the Communist Parties from around the world formed International Brigades to fight Franco's fascism. Communists formed the League Against War and Fascism rallying progressive writers and artists to oppose the Nazis. Admiration for Stalin and adherence to ideological Marxism-Leninism was widespread among the most vehement anti-racists and anti-fascists. BreadTube seeks to obscure this widely recognized historical reality and equate Communists with the people they heroically resisted, like Hitler and the KKK.

Natalie Wynn is merely the trendsetter, but she has given birth to a whole layer of pathetic confusion and childlike thought conformity. Across BreadTube, accusations of fascism grow on trees. Railroads are fascist. All Trump supporters are fascists. Neckties are fascist. Citing economic data is fascist. Quoting classical philosophers is fascist. Knowing enough about what fascism actually is in order to defend oneself against accusations of fascism is smoking gun proof you are a fascist.

By declaring all questioning of the status quo to be fascist, BreadTube is the best friend actual Nazis and fascists ever had. The result of their actions has been to channel millions of people who refuse to accept their mandated thought conformity into a position of interest or sympathy with actual fascism. Many who would have just been attracted to anti-war leftism or class struggle economics in the past have suddenly began exploring the teachings of Adolph Hitler, Julius Evola, and Gregor Strasser after being informed by the BreadTube internet circus that they are "Fascists" and "Red Browns."

Reader beware: In the aftermath of publication, buying, owning, or simply reading this book will be 100% confirmation to many BreadTubers that you are a fascist.

Such a disgusting trivialization of the millions who died in Hitler's gas chambers, and the millions more who died in the Second World War cannot even be imagined.

Chapter Four:
Understanding Left-Pessimism

In between his videos on suicidal ideation, self-harm, and childhood trauma, Matt "Thought Slime" decided to explain their analysis of modern capitalism: "When exactly do you think capital will be done making money? How much money is enough for the ultra-rich jackasses who already have most of it? We've long ago sailed past it because several of them own incalculable sums, so much that they could not spend it in a thousand lifetimes and yet they don't stop, despite the consequences, the human cost, the environmental cost, they keep going... There are only so many resources to be extracted from the earth until there aren't any left... They keep going forever, or more realistically, until they can't, and at that point we are doomed.... A human being intuitively understands that growth cannot continue forever, we understand the concept of finite resources... We the consumer, particularly, those of us in the west, bear some responsibility in this too. We buy shit we don't need and throw away shit other people could use."

The De-Growth Delusions

This view is inherently opposite of Marx's view. In Matt's view the problem is not that capitalism is holding back human progress and creativity, but rather that it is unleashing it. Like a neoliberal economist, Matt "Thought Slime" believes the delusion that somehow the system that leaves millions of people in poverty across the developing world, and increasingly drives first world workers into greater poverty and lower living standards, is not holding back human productivity. Like a free market economist, Matt "Thought Slime" believes capitalism is capable of creating endless growth, something the last 200 years of economic crises, wars, and chronic poverty despite technological advancement has clearly refuted. While Matt accept the premise that capitalism is capable of creating endless growth, Matt thinks this is bad.

In their video championing "de-growth", Thought Slime argues that humans have gone too far. The problem isn't that working people are increasingly impoverished due to capitalism's inherent creation of poverty amidst plenty, the problem is that average working people have too much stuff. As American workers are seeing their wages go down, their homes foreclosed, and their children condemned to a life of student debt, the problem is that they are still too comfortable. Thought Slime anticipates an ecological apocalypse unless human consumption can be urgently reduced. Matt insists their "degrowth" model is not the same as capitalist austerity.

This perspective is certainly not new. In 1972 a capitalist think-tank based in Italy called "The Club of Rome" published a document called *The Limits to Growth*. Jimmy Carter's White House published a document called *The Global 2000 Report* making similar claims.

This has been the worldview of many of the wealthiest and most powerful capitalists for a long time. In 1798 British economist Robert Malthus published *An Essay on the Principle of Population* arguing that the birth rate naturally outstrips the food supply, and measures must be implemented to stop peasants and workers from breeding. The Rockefeller family was heavily involved in the Neo-Malthusian society, sponsoring the Birth Control League and pushing for the legalization of abortion and contraception.

It is the biggest capitalists, namely those associated with the "free trade" theories of Adam Smith and the British Empire that have pushed "degrowth." They sit at the top of the world, and do not want to lose their position. Human history and progress must be ended so they can remain permanently in their winning position. The world must remain poor and get poorer, so they can stay rich.

The imperialist wars of the last 70 years have largely been de-growth operations. Millions were killed in Vietnam and Korea in the hopes of preventing these countries from industrializing with socialist economies. Iraq and Libya, who had used state-run oil resources to fund industrialization and development have been reduced to poverty and chaos. China and Russia are hated by the western imperialists because they are no longer impoverished client states, but competitors selling their own oil, steel, and computer technology in competition with the monopolists.

"Human progress has gone too far! Stop it!" Scream the Wall Street ultra-rich from the boardrooms of JP Morgan Chase, Exxon Mobil, and Bank of America. Not only must the developing world remain poor, they proclaim, but living standards must also drop in the west. The industrial middle class that once made western imperialist homelands so stable must be reduced to lower living standards.

Marxists have always opposed and dissected this fallacious logic. Friedrich Engels described Malthus' concept of "overpopulation" as "the crudest, most barbarous theory that ever existed, a system of despair which struck down all those beautiful phrases about love thy neighbor and world citizenship." In *Theories of Surplus Value*, Marx wrote, "Malthus's theory of value gives rise to the whole doctrine of the necessity for continually rising unproductive consumption which this exponent of over-population (because of shortage of food) preaches so energetically… this theory, for its part, suits his purpose remarkably well—an apologia for the existing state of affairs in England, for landlordism, 'State and Church', pensioners, tax-gatherers, tenths, national debt, stock-jobbers, beadles, parsons and menial servants… Malthus also wishes to see the freest possible development of capitalist production, however only insofar as the condition of this development is the poverty of its main basis, the working classes, but at the same time he wants it to adapt itself to the 'consumption needs' of the aristocracy and its branches in State and Church, to serve as the material basis for the antiquated claims of the representatives of interests inherited from feudalism and the absolute monarchy. Malthus wants bourgeois production as long as it is not revolutionary, constitutes no historical factor of development but merely creates a broader and more comfortable material basis for the 'old' society."

In his economic notebooks, Marx showed how Malthus' conceptions of "unproductive consumers" were completely false, but served the interests of the wealthy people who had commissioned his work. Marx wrote: "Malthus's book On Population was a lampoon directed against the French Revolution and the contemporary ideas of reform in England (Godwin, etc.). It was an apologia for the poverty of the working classes. The theory was plagiarized from Townsend and others. His Essay on Rent was a piece of polemic writing in support of the landlords against industrial capital. Its theory was taken from Anderson. His Principles of Political Economy was a polemic work written in the interests of the capitalists against the workers and in the interests of the aristocracy, Church, tax-eaters, toadies, etc., against the capitalists. Its theory was taken from Adam Smith. Where he inserts his own inventions, it is pitiable."

What is the inherent flaw regarding the logic of "limited resources"? This logic fails to take into account that the way human beings interact with resources has constantly been in a state of change. Across Africa, minerals are being extracted and sold at high value currently, when just several decades ago they were worthless. Computer chip technology has rendered them very valuable. The long predicted "peak oil" scenario in which petroleum would run out causing a global catastrophe never panned out, because new methods of extracting oil, from deep sea drilling to hydraulic fracking have been invented.

The current fossil fuel economy is certainly unsustainable and creating a global crisis of climate change, but the solution is moving to a more efficient and sustainable energy source, the most promising hope for which is nuclear fusion. For this reason, China and Russia have called for international cooperation for

Fusion research, and China has announced its intent to mine the rare isotope helium-3 from the Moon.

The way human beings interact with resources must change, no doubt about it. But the pessimistic notion that the human race must "de-grow" is frightening and unrealistic. As Friedrich Engels noted: "the animal merely uses its environment, and brings about changes in it simply by its presence; man by his changes makes it serve his ends, masters it. This is the final, essential distinction between man and other animals, and once again it is labor that brings about this distinction." Human beings are tool-makers and inventors, constantly changing how they interact with their

Many Anarchists and environmentalists put forward the notion that somehow growth and economic progress are bad, and societies should be reduced to lower living standards amid efforts to control the population.

environment, more efficiently forcing it to serve us and expand our life expectancy and quality of being.

Marxism seeks for the population to expand and for living standards to rise. In fact, the transition from the lower stage to the higher stage of Communism is rooted in the ability of a centrally planned economy to vastly increase the productive forces. In his *Critique of the Gotha Program* Marx explained that the ultimate goal of total equality and a stateless, classless world was only possible with vast material abundance. Marx wrote: "In the higher phase of Communist society, after the enslaving subordination of the individual to the division of labor, and therewith also the antithesis between mental and physical labor, has vanished; after labor has become not only a means of life but life's prime want; after the productive forces have also increase with the all around development of the individual, and all the springs of co-operative wealth flow more abundantly — only then can the narrow horizon of bourgeois right be crossed in its entirety and society inscribe on its banners: from each according to his ability, to each according to his needs!"

Marx was pointing to the fundamental reality that inequality is rooted in scarcity. Class society, the state, oppressive relations, and patriarchy are all rooted in managing a society at a certain level of development. As society has become more abundant and living standards have become higher, the rigidity of less abundant times has somewhat eroded. No one spoke of "freedom of speech" in ancient times, because such a concept was simply inconsistent with a society at this technological level. Scarcity necessitates authoritarianism and hierarchy, and abundance and development loosens these restraints creating equality and freedom.

Marx brilliantly ripped to shreds the "liberal" ideology of the enlightenment, exposing that rights and liberties are not "natural" and "god-given" but rather correspond to the economic base of society. Only by creating a society of vast abundance, totally eradicating scarcity, can total freedom be attained, and only by having rational central planning of the economy can this level of abundance be created. As capitalism holds back technological progress with the irrational creation of poverty amid plenty and the crisis of overproduction, it prevents humanity from marching toward the ultimate vision of a high-tech classless society of freedom and abundance.

Socialism has always been a fundamentally optimistic political movement. It views human history as marching forward from hunter-gatherer civilization, to slavery and feudalism, to capitalism, with socialism (the lower stage of Communism) and the ultimate higher stage of Communism on the horizon.

This understanding of the state, hierarchies and the progressive trajectory of humanity toward great abundance is what makes Marxist historical materialism so valuable. In an age where right-wing figures like Jordan Peterson argue that hierarchies and inequality are just natural, it is essential to understand human social structures as reflective of an underlying economic base. As the underlying economic base changes, human relations also change. The family, the nature of government, the level of freedom and social mobility is not rooted in some "natural" way found in our DNA or created by divinity. These institutions have evolved throughout human history as human beings moved toward a greater state of material abundance. BreadTube obscures this and furthermore denounces human progress and technological advance, thus feeding the common right-wing delusions.

The agenda of the ultra-rich proclaiming that human progress must be stopped has repeatedly been inserted into the socialist movement. In the process of Bonapartism, in which capitalists utilize workers as their foot soldiers in a struggle to stabilize the capitalist economy utilizing the state, various pessimistic counter-gangs have been formed in order to hijack the passion and activism of those who would be revolutionaries.

Georges Sorel's "Birth Strike"

The French philosopher Georges Sorel was the first prominent leftist voice to break with this optimism, long considered essential in the socialist movement. Sorel wrote in his 1908 pamphlet *Reflections on Violence*: "It seems to me that the optimism of the Greek philosophers depended to a great extent on economic reasons; it probably arose in the rich and commercial urban populations who were able to regard the universe as an immense shop full of excellent things with which they could satisfy their greed. I imagine that Greek pessimism sprang from poor warlike tribes living in the mountains, who were filled with an enormous aristocratic pride, but whose material conditions were

The first to introduce a pessimistic worldview into Marxian circles was the French syndicalist theoretician Georges Sorel.

correspondingly poor… they explained their present wretchedness to them by relating catastrophes in which semi-divine former chiefs had succumbed to fate or the jealousy of the gods; the courage of the warriors might for the moment be unable to accomplish anything, but it would not always be so; the tribe must remain faithful to the old customs in order to be ready for great and victorious expeditions, which might very well take place in the near future."

Sorel openly attacked the concept of optimism, and as his thought influenced the Syndicalist current in Europe, he broke with much of the Marxian tradition and outlook. The primary difference that Sorel had with the French Marxists and Social-Democrats was their belief in building a mass organization. Sorel argued that instead of building a broad organization among the working class with roots in unions, community groups, and such, it was instead better to build a group of fanatical dedicated men who would engage in "heroism" through acts of violence. Sorel invoked the power of mythology in building effective mass movements, and drew heavily from the history of Greece and Rome when arguing how to build an ideal revolutionary organization to overturn capitalism.

At the time of his death in 1922, Georges Sorel was an enthusiastic admirer of both Vladimir Lenin and Benito Mussolini. Sorel believed that both Lenin's "Party of New Type" and Mussolini's Blackshirts proved that his model of a violent "heroic" counter-gang, as opposed to a mass party, was effective.

While no record of contact between Lenin and Sorel can be established, the fascist dictator Benito Mussolini was heavily influenced by Sorel's teachings. Mussolini had been the editor of a socialist newspaper in Italy, but he broke with Marxism and became a syndicalist and adherent of Sorel's teachings while living in Switzerland in 1902. Eventually, Mussolini formed the Fascist Party in 1919, synthesizing the teachings of Georges Sorel with the theories of Italian Futurist Filippo Tommaso Marinetti, Friedrich Nietzsche, and Plato, among other influences. However, he made it clear: "I owe most to Georges Sorel. This master of syndicalism by his rough theories of revolutionary tactics has contributed most to form the discipline, energy and power of the fascist cohorts."

Mussolini's blackshirt gangs seized control of Italy and established the fascist state at the famous March on Rome in October of 1922.

The Spanish Falangists, the fascist movement led by Francisco Franco that ruled Spain from 1939 to 1975, is also rooted in Sorel's Syndicalism. Franco and his allies were originally members of the "National Syndicalist" party of Spain, a group of Sorelians who supported the Spanish monarchy, arguing that mystical power of the throne could be used to mobilize the working class.

Taking lead from Sorel, Mussolini and Franco utilized anti-capitalist demagogy, but wrapped it in pessimism, looking backward to the supposed glory of archaic monarchies and nationalistic imagery while glorifying violence and destruction. One big aspect of this was opposing the expansion of the human race and embracing the concept of "overpopulation."

In the lead-up to the First World War, the Syndicalists and followers of Georges Sorel began arguing for a "Birth Strike." They argued, in Marxian terms, that having children would drive wages down by increasing competition for jobs. They furthermore argued that revolutionaries should not be upstanding working class community members, but rather a special elite group of dedicated fanatics who did not have time for the distraction of family life.

While the Marxist movement supported the right of women to contraception and abortion, it rejected the "Birth Strike." They understood that believing poverty was due to "overpopulation" was a fundamental break with Marx's economic teachings. Marx had vehemently argued against the concept of overpopulation, and exposed the demagogy of the originator of this concept, Robert Malthus.

When Georges Sorel and his proto-fascist Syndicalists proposed the "Birth Strike" this was a component of rejecting Marxism's optimism. It fit in with their reintroduction of organizing methods rooted in

The syndicalist groups influenced by Georges Sorel merged into the wider, right-wing, fascist current during the lead up to the Second World War.

mystical chivalry and love of violence rather than material need and solidarity.

More than a century after Sorel wrote, pessimism flows through almost all that the dominant BreadTube voices say and do. In their view, the world is on the brink of collapse unless there can be a reduction of consumption. The population is too large. Technology has advanced too much. The pessimism manifests itself beyond merely the doomsday and hopeless rhetoric. The excessive use of profanity, the celebration of drug use, the endless conversation about suicide and mental illness, the fixation on ugly and grotesque things such as feces, semen, urine, dirt, slime, self-harm and cathartic violence all fit with this worldview.

The fact that Matt "Thought Slime" narrates sarcastic, crude videos which often condemn the concept of economic growth or fixate on mental illness related topics, while standing in front of the image of a sewer dripping with green slime may not be an accident. Let us revisit a passage from Malthus' infamous 1798 piece *An Essay on the Principle of Population*: "All children who are born, beyond what would be required to keep up the population to a desired level, must necessarily perish, unless room be made for them by the death of grown persons.... Therefore ... we should facilitate, instead of foolishly and vainly endeavoring to impede, the operations of nature in producing this mortality; and if we dread this too frequent visitation of the horrid form of famine, we should sedulously encourage the other forms of destruction, which we compel nature to use. **Instead of recommending cleanliness to the poor, we should encourage contrary habits. In our towns we should make the streets narrower, crowd more people into the houses, and court the return of the plague. In the country, we should build our villages near stagnant pools, and particularly encourage settlement in all marshy and unwholesome situations.** But above all we should reprobate specific remedies for ravaging diseases; and restrain those benevolent, but much mistaken men, who have thought they are doing a service to mankind by protecting schemes for the total extirpation of particular disorders."

It is also worth noting that Sorelian pessimist and ex-socialist Benito Mussolini shared the fixation on feces and the cruel degrading humor of bullies, often found among BreadTube voices. One of Mussolini's favorite ways of punishing dissidents is described in Peter Carlson's 2016 article published on HistoryNet: "As Rogers studied Mussolini, he learned about the dictator's favorite disciplinary tool—castor oil. Blackshirts would seize a foe, rough him up, strap him to a chair, and pour the laxative down his throat. Once the fellow soiled himself, the Blackshirts would send him home sick, hurting, and humiliated."

The article describes how mainstream US media radio personality Will Rogers found this demented practice to be humorous and joked about it with the murderous fascist dictator while they bonded over Russophobia: "Rogers found this stratagem hilarious. 'I know of nothing that would lessen a man's political aspirations more than this,' he wrote. 'Just think of the possibilities not only in Italy but in our country.' ... Delighted that an American appreciated his torturous innovation, Mussolini elaborated. 'One fellow, he not so bad, we give him half-liter,' he said, laughing. 'Next fellow, he bad boy, we give him one liter.' Rogers asked Mussolini to sell him the recipe so he could dose U.S.

The fascist dictator Benito Mussolini was known for torturing Communists and political dissidents by inducing diarrhea with castor oil. US radio personality Will Rogers was highly amused by this tactic.

senators engaging in filibusters. Congressmen were 'not so bad,' Rogers added, so he'd give them only half a liter. The two men laughed. Rogers said he was going to Russia. 'Oh, Russia,' Mussolini said. 'You take recipe to Russia. Very good for Russia—castor oil. I give you free.' And they laughed again."

The pessimism also fits with another theme in Sorel's ideology, which is "the power of myth." While Marxists focused on seizing power, the Syndicalists rejected politics favoring only direct activism on the job between workers and employers. Syndicalists argued that a 'great general strike' in which all the workers of the world refused to work and seized their factories would end capitalism in one big dramatic battle. Sorel's writing argued that while this glorious apocalypse was unlikely to actually happen, the myth of it would inspire great revolutionary activism. In essence, Sorel foreshadowed the eventual emergence of post-modernism, saying truth does not really matter and that ideas, feelings, and "narratives" are more important than objective reality.

BreadTube voices generally argue that truth does not exist, and that the only positive role for revolutionaries to play is that of deconstruction if not outright destruction. This thinking follows the trajectory of anti-Marxist post-modernism, a trend directly linked to the Congress for Cultural Freedom and CIA covert efforts.

In the BreadTube perspective we find echoes of George Orwell and Ayn Rand's post-WW2 middle class dystopias. In the presented view, all principles which people may give their lives to are merely totalitarian scams. All heroes who people may idealize are hypocrites and demagogues. All statues must be torn down. All states must be smashed. All hope is naive. All passion and love between people is weakness. The individual stands against the world, the rest of the human race, the vulgar mob that would take away his sacred isolation.

There is no real vision of a post-capitalist world to strive for beyond "start a cooperative pencil factory," so instead BreadTube voices merely celebrate the libidinal release of tearing down the current world in an explosion of rage. The glory is found in memes such as "punch a Nazi" or taking gleeful pleasure in the suffering of a person deemed to be privileged. One identity politics oriented group called Black Hammer announced that Anne Frank, the victim of the Nazi holocaust whose eloquent diary was published in the post-war years, was a "Karen." The group has announced it intends to burn copies of *The Diary of Anne Frank* as a fundraiser for its efforts to build a city in Colorado in which no whites are permitted.

Sexual Freedom and Left-Pessimism

Sexual frustration seems to be a big component of Left pessimism, as its most infamous recruit demonstrates.

Margaret Sanger was a primary financial backer of the Industrial Workers of the World and was a leading figure in the Socialist Party of New York City. Sanger associated with a number of wealthy left-wing intellectuals in New York City in the early years of the 20th Century, including John Reed, Emma Goldman, Max Eastman and Upton Sinclair. Sanger led fundraising efforts to support the strikes of textile workers in New Jersey and eventually launched her own magazine *The Woman Rebel.*

Sanger was a Marxist, but central in all things was her belief in sexual freedom. Marxism promised to liberate women from patriarchy and thus create a world of "free love" in which sexual desires would no longer be restrained, and this seemed to be the primary appeal of left-wing politics for Margaret Sanger. The slogan frequently used in her publication was "No Gods, No Masters," a phrase that remains popular with anarchists.

After calling for the assassination of John D. Rockefeller and facing criminal charges for distributing birth control, Sanger fled the United States for Britain in 1914. In Britain, she began to associate with the Neo-Malthusian Society. Charles Vickery Drysdale was the founder of the Malthusian League. The League was comprised of a group of wealthy British people who believed birth control and abortion could reduce the human population. Opinion such as Sanger's

Marxism began to fade following the Russian Revolution of 1917. The Soviet Union did not become the free love paradise of sexual liberation she had hoped for. However, Sanger's new friends in the British Neo-Malthusian society were fully committed to legalizing birth control and abortion, as well as promoting pornography. The very Rockefeller oligarchs whom she had previously threatened soon gave her financial backing. With her legal troubles conveniently resolved, Sanger returned to the US and established the first birth control clinic in New York City.

Sanger denounced Marxism in scathing polemics, announcing that the problem was not capitalism but simply humanity's drive to procreate and expand: "Discontented workers may rally to Marxism because it places the blame for their misery outside of themselves and depicts their conditions as the result of a capitalistic conspiracy, thereby satisfying that innate tendency of every human being to shift the blame to some living person outside himself, and because it strengthens his belief that his sufferings and difficulties may be overcome by the immediate amelioration of his economic environment. In this manner, psychologists tell us, neuroses and inner compulsions are fostered. No true solution is possible, to continue this analogy, until the worker is awakened to the realization that the roots of his malady lie deep in his own nature, his own organism, his own habits. To blame everything upon the capitalist and the environment produced by capitalism is to focus attention upon merely one of the elements of the problem. The Marxian too often forgets that before there was a capitalist there was exercised the unlimited reproductive activity of mankind, which produced the first overcrowding, the first want. This goaded humanity into its industrial frenzy, into warfare and theft and slavery. Capitalism has not created the lamentable state of affairs in which the world now finds itself. It has grown out of them, armed with the inevitable power to take advantage of our swarming, spawning millions."

Like most contemporary environmentalists, Sanger concluded that individual workers and the very creative nature of humanity was the problem, not capitalism. As Sanger joined in with the wealthiest capitalists to

After abandoning Marxism in favor of Malthusianism, Margaret Sanger began courting support from racists such as the Ku Klux Klan.

reduce the human population, she began to espouse genocidal racism, speaking at Ku Klux Klan rallies. Lothrop Stoddard, one of the most outspoken Eugenicists and White Supremacists of the 1920s, served on the American Birth Control League's National Board. In personal correspondence, Sanger talked of the need to cultivate Black ministers to promote birth control, and passingly admitted some rather horrific intentions, writing: "We do not want word to go out that we want to exterminate the Negro population and the minister is the man who can straighten out that idea if it ever occurs to any of their more rebellious members."

In 1921, a speech from Margaret Sanger specifically condemned working class and low-income people for being religious and having many children, proclaiming: "There is no doubt in the minds of all thinking people that the procreation of this group should be stopped."

When the Great Depression hit and mass hunger and starvation took place across the United States, Sanger's former comrades formed Hunger Marches and Unemployment Councils demanding economic relief. Chanting "Work or Wages now!" the Communist Party forced the Roosevelt administration to create the Works Progress Administration, Social Security and Unemployment Insurance. Sanger doubled-down on her position, blaming the economic crisis on overpopulation and condemning efforts to feed the hungry masses. Sanger's book *The Pivot of Civilization* condemned helping the poor, saying that doing so "encourages the healthier and more normal sections of the world to shoulder the burden of unthinking and indiscriminate fecundity of others; which brings with it, as I think the reader must agree, a dead weight of human waste. Instead of decreasing and aiming to eliminate the stocks that are most detrimental to the future of the race and the world, it tends to render them to a menacing degree dominant."

Planned Parenthood, the successor to Sanger's Birth Control League, often claims that Sanger was not herself a racist, but simply appealed to racism in the hopes of promoting women's right to contraception. Sanger may not have harbored consciously racist views, but she was very openly a Malthusian. She believed the problem was not capitalism, but the working people themselves and their desire to procreate and improve their lives. The goal was not a world of greater abundance and prosperity, but rather some kind of great correction that would kill off the "useless eaters" and throw the world back into balance.

Orgasmic Politics

Margaret Sanger's departure from Marxism, trading socialism for sex, follows a common pattern of Synthetic Leftism. Many deviations from scientific socialism appear intoxicated by a carnal undertone.

Rather than seeking a healthy society of sustainable growth and human progress, the goal is a cathartic explosion of destruction and vengeance.

At the time feudalism was toppled in Europe, the Roman Catholic Church was obviously a primary target of the emerging bourgeois revolutionaries. However, many of the mercantile capitalists and conspiring rationalists embraced pre-Christian European religions and mysticism rather than science. Pantheism, sun-worship, Odinism, and the alchemical tradition was popular among the anti-feudal revolutionaries who often organized themselves into secret societies like the Freemasons or the Bavarian Illuminati.

In the mid 1800s, as the new "leisure class" of capitalists with lots of free time was created, a trend rightly called "salon culture" came to dominate intellectual circles. A variety of different forms of flim-flam pseudo-intellectual entertainment emerged to alleviate the boredom of the privileged. Freudian Psychoanalysis, the Occultist teachings of Aleister Crowley, Hypnotism, and various spiritualist movements eventually emerged from this cultural trend.

Unlike Marxism, these trends all seemed to emphasize the importance of the individual rather than the collective fate of humanity. Furthermore, unlike Marxism, the various occult trends did not predict a transition to a higher stage of civilization, but rather an explosive destruction that would return humans to a state of harmony with nature.

In his book *Civilization and its Discontents,* Freud argued that civilization was not a worthwhile endeavor, as the impulse for aggression was natural. Christianity is lambasted for urging "love thy neighbor as yourself"

The influence of salon culture and various charlatans such as Aleister Crowley, who pander to the idol rich, has been a longstanding curse on left-wing politics. Marx urged his followers to get beyond such circles and to the laboring masses who produce society's wealth.

which Freud deems impossible, leading to endless guilt and shame. Allister Crowley told his followers that "Do As Thou Wilt Shall Be the Whole of the Law," and that through his rituals and counseling, he could help them discover their inner will and true desires so they could be pursued and satisfied.

Wagner's Ring Cycle, a series of four operas completed in 1874, dazzled audiences throughout Europe. The opera was not for the working class but for the leisure class. Not surprisingly, Wagner's magnum opus contains similar themes to the revolutionary intelligentsia. The plot and characters were derived from Germanic mythology. The final opera concludes with Brünhilde, mourning her slain hero Siegfried, mounting a horse and riding it into his funeral pyre as an act of passionate suicide. The fire then spreads and the entire world soon bursts into flames in a climactic apocalypse. The natural beauty of the Rhine River is all that remains.

The Revolutionary Intelligentsia, young students and intellectuals drawn to left-wing politics, was and remains heavily stamped by the influence of Salon Culture. Many of those who embraced Marxism, Socialism, or Anarchism were among the same privileged strata where Freud, Crowley, and various charlatans and performers made their rounds.

In BreadTube politics, much like 1960s counterculture, one finds a heavy representation of the salon culture's remnants. The journey of the individual to discover what they truly desire and who they truly are is very much the focus. The fulfillment of sexual desires and liberation from restraints on sexual impulses, as well as impulses toward aggression and resentment against authority, is also central. There is a condescending fascination with primitive cultures believing they are somehow purer than the modern world corrupted by technology.

While efforts to conceal it have largely been successful, the age of information technology has allowed the US public to see more clearly that the occultist, apocalyptic, hypersexual, and pantheist tendencies are very much alive among the ruling elites of American capitalism. US politicians and business

Among the rich, mystical rituals and occultism remain popular. Many prominent political and business figures in the United States gather at an exclusive nude resort called the Bohemian Grove in California.

elites are part of secret societies like the Order of Skulls and Bones at Yale, and they gather in nude resorts like the Bohemian Grove. Al Gore and many prominent figures in the Democratic Party received spiritual advice from Marilyn Ferguson, an occult guru based in Southern California who published a bizarre political screed called *The Aquarian Conspiracy* in 1980. The book calls for a mass spiritual awakening. It lays out an individual process for "personal transformation" that follows the brainwashing patterns developed by American intelligence agencies, promoting hallucinogenic drugs, hypnosis, and other methods.

Ferguson describes California as the center of her "conspiracy" and lists several CIA linked academic think tanks such as the Stanford Research Institute as being onboard. It was later revealed that the Stanford Research Institute spent decades conducting CIA-funded research into telekinesis and other paranormal beliefs, and was also involved in project MK-ULTRA, the CIA drug program.

The pessimism, sex obsession, anti-growth politics of BreadTube clearly have deep roots. They are not the personal innovation of Vaush, Thought Slime, Contrapoints, or any other shallow internet personality. But these are not the politics of the working class.

These are the politics of the ultra-rich who find amid their splendorous existence that something is missing. They want to dig into their personal psyches, discover and unleash their sexual desires, and fantasize about existing in a more primitive state of being where "harmony with nature" would mean less restraints on their impulses. They seek to explore the depths of their personalities and perhaps overcome some heavy subconscious guilt that flows from living at the top of a global empire. They seek the thrill of a cathartic explosion that will correct the injustices of the world, putting everything back into balance.

Beyond whatever psychological motivations, there are the direct economic ones. The pessimistic politics represent the interests of those who already sit at the top of the world economy; ultra-monopolists who say

Occultist guru Marily Ferguson served as the spiritual advisor to Al Gore and other prominent politicians. Her ties to CIA research at the Stanford Research Institute were quite visible.

growth must end because they are already on top. The oil banking elite sees nuclear power and human progress beyond fossil fuels as a threat to their global order. For them, Climate Change can only mean that humans have gone too far, and a mass reduction of the population and consumption is needed.

The working class, however, in its desire to build and construct, solving problems by driving forward human progress, has a completely different worldview. Unlike the optimistic Marxists who lead China and the Bolivarian countries, BreadTube does not serve the march of humanity toward freedom from the irrationality of greed. In its pessimism and destructive mindset, BreadTube serves imperialism.

Conclusion: The Conditions Themselves Call Out...

Louis Bonaparte's regime that seized control of France in 1851 did not work to bring the working class to power. Its aim was to stabilize French capitalism on behalf of one section of the capitalist class. Karl Marx described the coalition the military dictator built for himself.

Marx wrote: "On the pretext of founding a benevolent society, the lumpen proletariat of Paris had been organized into secret sections, each section led by Bonapartist agents, with a Bonapartist general at the head of the whole. Alongside decayed roués with dubious means of subsistence and of dubious origin, alongside ruined and adventurous offshoots of the bourgeoisie, were vagabonds, discharged soldiers, discharged jailbirds, escaped galley slaves, swindlers, mountebanks, lazzarone, pickpockets, tricksters, gamblers, pimps, brothel keepers, porters, literati, organ grinders, ragpickers, knife grinders, tinkers, beggars — in short, the whole indefinite, disintegrated mass, thrown hither and thither, which the French call la bohème; from this kindred element Bonaparte formed the core of the Society of December 10. A "benevolent society" — insofar as, like Bonaparte, all its members felt the need of benefiting themselves at the expense of the laboring nation. This Bonaparte, who constitutes himself chief of the lumpenproletariat, who here alone rediscovers in mass form the interests which he personally pursues, who recognizes in this scum, offal, refuse of all classes the only class upon which he can base himself unconditionally, is the real Bonaparte, the Bonaparte sans phrase. An old, crafty roué, he conceives the historical life of the nations and their performances of state as comedy in the most vulgar sense, as a masquerade in which the grand costumes, words, and postures merely serve to mask the pettiest knavery."

This passage from Marx, containing plenty of outdated and unfamiliar terminology, is essential to understanding BreadTube. The Merriam-Webster dictionary defines *roues* as "men devoted to a life of sensual pleasure." *Literati* are "well-educated people who are interested in literature." *Mountebanks* refers to "persons who deceive others in order to trick them out of their money." *Lazzaroni* is an Italian term referring to the desperately poor organized into gangs, often described as "street people under a chief." When Marx describes "the whole indefinite, disintegrated mass, thrown hither and thither, which the French call la bohème" it can easily be understood that what he describing is counter-culture ("bohemians") elements.

Marx describes this counter-gang amassed by Louis Bonaparte as "benefiting themselves at the expense of the laboring nation." This lumpenproletariat according to Marx is separate from those who lay the basis of the Communist revolution. The proletariat, the class with nothing to lose but their chains and the world to win, who sit at the center of the Marxist narrative of world history, are not organ grinders, pickpockets, and literati. Rather, they are the broad masses, the working class. The *real* proletariat are the millions and millions of people who spend their days working in order to pay their bills, feed their children, and hopefully retire in old age. The proletariat are not grifters, leeching wealth from the society around, but rather the class that produces the wealth with their labor power.

When looking over BreadTube's various personalities, we can clearly see modern incarnations of the elements Marx describes in the coup d'état assembled by the original Bonapartist. It appears that in order to beat back Donald Trump and the rebellion of the New Right, Biden assembled his own "society of December 10th." Among its ranks we find roues (Vaush), literati (Contrapoints), mountebanks (Thought Slime), lazzaroni, vagabonds and discharged soldiers (Antifa), the 21st century's digital "Brothel Keepers" and pornography industry, the marijuana and hallucinogen lobby, all of them "with dubious means of subsistence and of dubious origin", as they collect money from anonymous sources on Patreon and benefit from the convenient love of the social media algorithms.

And who do they see as their enemy? The laboring nation. While they do not call out Falun Gong, the Israel Lobby, the Miami Cubans, or other foreign policy interest groups who marched on January 6th, they single out the low-income white workers with their Confederate flags as the target.

It is certainly right to condemn the use of the Confederate Flag, a symbol of a pro-slavery uprising backed by the British empire and Wall Street insurance cartels, but this is not their real grievance with Middle America. The crime of middle America is that they do not accept the "de-growth" presently being forced on them. They do not accept their kids dying from opioids and being locked in for-profit prisons, facing a lifetime of low wages. They do not accept the factories closing down and good paying jobs disappearing as we transition to a global low wage economy. They do not accept the idea that they the working people are merely evil privileged Eurosettlers who deserve to be poorer as retribution for historical and ongoing injustices. They do not accept that Silicon Valley should rule over all society determining what ideas are and are not acceptable in the discourse. They do not accept the post-modernist commandment that Jesus Christ and his teachings of kindness and brotherhood should be replaced with academic moral relativism, Allister Crowley's "Do As Thou Wilt" or Ayn Rand's "Virtue of Selfishness." They do not see human solidarity as inherently totalitarian and fascist. They do not see the celebrated individualism of a few lumpen content creators, who are triggered by class struggle rhetoric and popular will, as worthy of holding back all humanity's dreams of a better future.

Let us be reminded of Lenin's famous essay *Imperialism and the Split in Socialism*, where he ripped to shreds the social chauvinists who dominated the various social democratic parties of the world, but ended by urging genuine revolutionaries not to abandon their task: "Neither we nor anyone else can calculate precisely what portion of the proletariat is following and will follow the social-chauvinists and opportunists. This will be revealed only by the struggle, it will be definitely decided only by the socialist revolution. ....**And it is therefore our duty, if we wish to remain socialists to go down *lower and deeper*, to the real masses; this is the whole meaning and the whole purport of the struggle against opportunism**. By exposing the fact that the opportunists and social-chauvinists are in reality betraying and selling the interests of the masses, that they are defending the temporary privileges of a minority of the workers, that they are the vehicles of bourgeois ideas and influences, that they are really allies and agents of the bourgeoisie, we teach the masses to appreciate their true political interests, to fight for socialism and for the revolution through all the long and painful vicissitudes of imperialist wars and imperialist armistices."

The broad masses of Americans are full of anger and ripe for rebellion against the same forces from which China, Russia, Nicaragua, Cuba, Venezuela, Vietnam, Iran, Syria and many other countries have already broken free. The ultra-rich class of multinational oligarchs and their "great reset" would destroy the lives of the American proletariat and drive it down to the third world conditions, all to facilitate the high tech, low wage economy that no longer deems their labor power to be valuable.

It is not only white Americans who are ready to rebel. The Black Lives Matter uprising. The refusal of Minister Louis Farrakhan to support Hillary Clinton. The rise of Black and Chicano Nationalism. The increased Asian American political awareness. The massive demonstrations against US complicity in Israeli crimes by Arab Americans. These all show rising opposition to the Wall Street Silicon Valley New World Order among all different strata of the American working class.

With the voices purporting to represent the Marxist movement having turned their back on them, the rising anger of the American working class manifests itself in many confused ways. Conspiracy theories, libertarianism, and other delusions take the place of scientific socialism. This can only be resolved by conscious revolutionaries abandoning the protest cages and liberal "safe spaces" and spreading the liberating truth in places it has never been heard. **The future of socialism is getting out of "the movement" and to the masses.**

Donald Trump attempted to hijack this rising discontent, and his racist demagogy, appealing to bigotry and free market "might is right" neoliberal thinking certainly took hold. But Trump failed because he was unable to resolve the crisis. The problems Trump claimed to address are rooted in a society of which he is merely a creation, and of whose ideology he is a vocal promoter. The problems facing US society are not cultural. They do not flow from a lack of Gender Studies courses or anti-racist trainings in workplaces. They will not be resolved with employee stock ownership programs or kneeling ceremonies on Capitol Hill.

The only solution to the crisis facing US society is a government of action that will fight for working families. The broad masses of people, who have been misdirected by many phonies of both the right and the synthetic left, must demand swift government action to resolve the crisis. The banks, factories, industries, and all centers of economic power must be controlled by popular power. The chaos of the market must be eliminated, and a rational, centrally planned economy must emerge to replace the nightmare of capitalism in order to ensure that growth and human progress are unending.

The awakening of the American proletariat will be a gradual, difficult process, but it is the only way in which the present contradictions and the failures of decaying imperialism can be resolved. As Marx reminded us in his pamphlet on Louis Bonaparte: "Proletarian revolutions, like those of the nineteenth century, constantly criticize themselves, constantly interrupt themselves in their own course, return to the apparently accomplished, in order to begin anew; they deride with cruel thoroughness the half-measures, weaknesses, and paltriness of their first attempts, seem to throw down their opponents only so the latter may draw new strength from the earth and rise before them again more gigantic than ever, recoil constantly from the indefinite colossalness of their own goals — until a situation is created which makes all turning back impossible, and the conditions themselves call out: Hic Rhodus, hic salta! (Here's The Rose, Now Dance!)"

Appendix #1:
4-Point Plan to Rescue the Country – Center for Political Innovation

We, the Center for Political Innovation, see that urgent measures are needed to save the country from the disaster created by the greed of billionaire bankers and capitalists. We put forward this 4-point plan:

1. A Mass Mobilization to Rebuild the Country

Now is the time to hire the millions of unemployed at union wages. Put them to work rebuilding the roads, bridges, water treatment facilities, power plants, schools, and hospitals of the country. High speed railway must connect the Midwest and South to more prosperous regions. The universities must be revamped so once again we are churning out the world's greatest scientists and engineers.

A brain trust of the smartest minds must be assembled in order to lay out a detailed 5 year economic plan. The public must be mobilized to carry it out with the full support of the country's resources.

2. Public Ownership of Natural Resources

It has become clear that big corporations and banks are not trustworthy in their management of America's oil, natural gas, coal, timber, and other natural resources. As communities across the country fall into greater poverty, Wall Street monopolists enrich themselves from the natural wealth of American soil. Nationalization of these resources will end the budget deficit. The profits from America's wealth must go to the country overall, not into the pockets of a few bankers. Popular power will be far more capable of managing these resources in a sustainable and eco-friendly way to ensure a better future in the face of the looming climate crisis.

3. Public Control of Banking

Speculation, money created from money with no real added value, hangs as a curse over the US economy. The Bible, the Torah, the Koran and every major religion historically has forbidden the lending of money at interest because it creates an ultra-rich creditor class, bringing the problem of monopolistic stagnation; extreme centralization of wealth in the hands of a few.

The lending of money should no longer be carried out for profit, but should be done by communities and the country overall at the local, state, and federal level.

In place of the financial sector, a National Bank as well as many state and local banks should be created. Credit should be assigned in accordance with an overall economic plan, securing long term growth and development. Interest should be paid back into the public budget, lifting the burden of taxation from working families.

4. An Economic Bill of Rights

In his final State of the Union address, President Franklin Roosevelt proposed an Economic Bill of Rights. The right to a job, housing, education, and healthcare must be added to the US constitution. No one in the country should be left hungry while so much wealth exists. No one should be homeless in a country with millions of empty houses and apartments. All who can work should be hired to do useful work building a better America. Education should be considered a necessity for maintaining an informed population and healthy country.

Conclusion

The crisis facing the United States, exacerbated by the pandemic, is rooted in the capitalist system. The US has embraced insane, libertarian neoliberal economics. The setting up of prisons for profit, schools for profit, and private military contractors, all while reducing the public budget and decreasing the quality of life for the population. The public is viewed by the ruling elite as an obnoxious horde to be controlled and managed. The United States and the rest of the world are being reduced to greater poverty, in order to ensure that a clique of big bankers and international monopolies can stay at the top of a global high-tech economy. The danger of a new world war hangs over the USA, as it threatens countries like China, Russia, Iran, and Venezuela.

We, the Center for Political Innovation, reject this vision for "de-growth," a 21st Century Dark Age. Human creativity must be unleashed to build a better future. This 4-point plan is intended to move the USA toward a rational socialist planned economy.

America was founded on slavery and genocide of native people, but the legacy of ugly wars and racism are not the only side of this country. Within US history one can find a long history of progressives. Abolitionists, suffragists, labor unionists, peace activists, innovators, and optimists are just as much a part of America's history as the war mongers and monopolists. This progressive side of the American people must be awakened in order to reconquer political power and drive out the war-makers and bankers.

The current economic crisis is giving birth to a new generation of young people who are engaging with left-wing and revolutionary ideas in the hopes of saving the country from the nightmare of capitalism. Those who feel a sense of responsibility, patriotism, and morality must take history into their hands. The time is now.

We Need a Government of Action To Fight for Working Families!

Appendix #2:
Note on the Political
Development of the Author

It is necessary to put this book in proper context by providing some insight into the background of the author and my experiences with Marxism and the leftist milieu.

I first became interested in Marxism as a teenager growing up in rural Ohio. In a deeply conservative small town, my opposition to the US invasion of Iraq and my non-conforming personality forced me to begin investigating political topics. My mother was a librarian who was organized into the Service Employees International Union and went on strike with other public employees to demand better workplace conditions. Walking the picket lines with her as a child also probably influenced my development, as did my parents' love for traditional folk music, much of which contained leftist themes.

Regardless, as I began studying Marxism, I found the tone of *The Communist Manifesto* and other texts to be very inspiring, despite the fact that I struggled to figure out what these texts actually meant in an atmosphere of total confusion and disinformation about socialism.

In 1999, as a 12-year-old child, I visited Ecuador with my father. We came to Quito amid an economic crisis. The neoliberal reforms imposed by the IMF and World Bank, compounded with crop failures and the collapse of the Asian markets, all resulted in a devastating episode of malnutrition and mass poverty. Hundreds of thousands of people died or fled the country as Ecuador's economy collapsed in a "man-made famine" created by Neoliberalism. Seeing these extreme conditions and economic devastation at such a young age, despite not understanding their real origin, most likely pointed me toward an anti-imperialist mindset.

In the aftermath of 9/11, I studied the work of Noam Chomsky, Howard Zinn, and Ward Churchill, and became aware of the ugly history of US military interventions. I had been led to believe the US went around the world fighting for freedom and overthrowing dictators. I soon learned that the reality of US foreign policy in South America, Africa, Asia, and elsewhere was quite contrary to the propaganda I had been spoon fed. I reached out to the Communist sects that operated in Cleveland, the nearest major US city, and started reading their publications.

It was discovering the works of William Z. Foster and other leaders of the US Communist Party during the 1930s that truly opened my eyes to understanding Marxism. The literature of the Communist Party USA from this era put forward Marxist-Leninist concepts in very plain language. I began to actively devour texts published in the 1920s, 30s, 40s, and 50s. They gave me clear answers in a way texts written in more recent decades when academics and middle class elements dominated leftist discourse, did not.

As a college student I was able to become politically active, and was quickly swept into a small Maoist group that operated in Cleveland. They put me to work selling their weekly newspaper on college campuses and in African-American neighborhoods. I discovered that I was very good at selling newspapers, and my self-education and study enabled me to engage with people about socialist concepts very effectively.

As I sold newspapers on a regular basis, I learned that the strongest arguments in favor of socialism were economic ones. Socialism would ensure that people had jobs, healthcare, and education. Socialism would ensure rational use of resources. However, as I began making these arguments, the elderly Maoists I worked with informed me this was "economism" and thus unacceptable. According to them, the argument for socialism was about "liberation" and "ending oppressive relations." They informed me that the jobs and wealth enjoyed by many Americans was created by exploitation of the third world and our goal was not necessarily to expand it.

These Maoists shunned labor activism, and having denounced China in 1976, had no relationship with any existing socialist or anti-imperialist countries. They focused on agitation around the issue of police brutality and civil liberties, and often their rhetoric was laced with profanity and violent imagery. I soon drifted away from them.

In 2007, I joined the Workers World Party (WWP), seeing that the group's rhetoric was more rooted in class struggle and that the group was supportive of Cuba, China, Venezuela, and other countries seeking to build socialism around the world.

The 2008 Crisis of Capitalism

As a college student, I wrote articles for WWP's weekly newspaper, and attended demonstrations in the Cleveland area against the imperialist wars, the mistreatment of prisoners, and police brutality. I also convened study groups about Marxism on my college campus and at a local leftist bookstore. Occasionally our branch of 5 WWP members hosted national party leaders to speak in Cleveland when they were visiting Ohio. I distributed WW newspapers throughout the city, and worked hard to try and promote the organization and its literature.

During the first months of my involvement with WWP, I had the opportunity to interact a number of times and receive a mild amount of mentorship from Leslie Feinberg. Leslie was a working-class Communist from Buffalo and WWP member who is often noted as the first openly Transgender activist in US history. Leslie's works such as *Stone Butch Blues* and *Transgender Warriors* are treasured by trans theorists and academics. She became ill with Lyme disease shortly afterward. Leslie made a point of instructing me about the many unwritten rules of WWP's internal procedures, as well as engaging with me about the political line of several articles I submitted to the WW newspaper.

I received a large amount of direct mentorship from an elderly woman in Cleveland who had been a founding member of Workers World Party in 1959. Born in 1928, Frances Dostal had been a member of the Socialist Workers Party prior to the split that established WWP. Both of her parents had been members of the Communist Party in Brooklyn, New York, and she had spent her childhood in the 1930s attending Young Pioneer summer camps and Marxist after school programs.

Frances had a way of engaging with people and explaining Marxist-Leninist concepts in popular language that is very rare in our time, but was common when she was growing up. The language she used reminded me of Woody Guthrie songs, and was very much a remnant of time before anti-populism had infected left-wing politics during the 1960s. This was the language of William Z. Foster, Gus Hall, Eugene Debs, Elizabeth Gurly Flynn, Ben Davis, Harry Haywood, and the other activists of another era, who built a serious revolutionary organization aimed at reaching the broad masses and building a socialist America.

In 2008 the US economy crashed, and I became thoroughly convinced that Marxism should not merely be a hobby or a personal indulgence. I studied Marx's Capital and other texts and became convinced that the financial crisis was rooted in overproduction.

During this period, WWP began to encourage its members to study the achievements of the Communist Party during the 1930s, the unemployment councils and hunger marches. My already existing interest in this history peaked, and I began to devour books on the history of the Communist Party, the history of Trotskyism, Marxist economics, the history of the Black Liberation movement, and all else.

I could not understand why my enthusiasm was not matched by the older party members. They urged me to just find a job and set up a normal life, and just treat Marxism as a kind of side hobby. However, I could see very well that the moment was full of great potential, and that I needed to throw my entire life into organizing the mass socialist movement that was needed. I became well known as a Communist activist in Cleveland after video recording an instance of police brutality outside of Collinwood High School. I was profiled in Cleveland Scene magazine as "The Communist Next Door."

In Cleveland, I directly observed the activism of an organization called Black on Black Crime, Inc., directed by Art Mccoy. The organization had a Black Nationalist orientation, but it functioned as an organizing center of the African-American community on Cleveland's East Side. Each Wednesday its meetings had 50 to 70 people attending to discuss issues like traffic light cameras, hospital closings, police brutality, and housing affordability. The organization often negotiated gang truces to stop violence between rival criminal organizations.

As I have studied the Communist movement around the world, I realize now that Black on Black Crime, Inc. was the closest thing to what functioning Communist Parties and anti-imperialist mass movements are in other countries. The basis of effective Marxist and revolutionary organizations, be they Bolivarian, Baathist, or Marxist-Leninist, is their base among the population and their ability to serve as centers of the community. During the 1930s, the Communist Party USA certainly played this role, and the Black Panther Party did during the 1960s and 70s. Currently no Communist grouping in the United States functions in this manner as an embodiment of community power on a local level, and this is the very essence of the weakness of American leftism.

Living in Cleveland was simply unsustainable for me after finishing college amid the financial crisis. After working in many gas stations, holding many short term low wage jobs, selling my blood plasma, and struggling to get by, I finally did like many of my peers and I migrated to the East Coast. I ultimately relocated to New York City in December of 2010, and continued my activism in WWP's national office.

The amount of dysfunction I observed was massive. Hundreds of copies of the weekly newspaper were thrown into the garbage each week. Phone calls from prospective members asking to join were never answered. While the party's rank and file contained many lifelong dedicated Marxist activists, the party's so-called leaders seemed completely uninterested in ideology and theory.

The unelected clique at WWP's head focused on staging rallies around whatever the latest trendy liberal cause was, and were often deeply unaware even of WWP's own history and positions on issues like gun control. Watching these ignorant "activists" incoherently present Marxist concepts I had worked hard to understand, and preside over the decay of an already nearly dead organization was infuriating for me. It was simply not permitted to disagree with these leaders or try to correct the party from its course of deterioration.

Accusations of being "un-comradely" and "working to undermine faith in our leaders," often laced in allegations of racism, sexism, or homophobia were used to silence all who challenged the rule of a small clique of very non-ideological individuals. The rank and file of the party contained many dedicated, ideological baby boomers who had learned to submit and obey over the course of decades of declining influence. The clique who sat at the top of the group were "activists" who had been bequeathed the organization after the death of Sam Marcy, the party's charismatic founder. They could not be voted out or removed.

WWP remains like many of the Marxist-Leninist parties of the world today, a piece of wreckage from the Cold War-era. It is stuck in the past, with a worldview and strategy that do not fit contemporary events. With an outdated worldview that its leaders did not really understand or care about updating, WWP tailed after whatever the liberal activists and labor bureaucracy was doing. They hoped that they could maneuver into securing the permit, setting up the stage, and thus being "the vanguard" of "the movement."

As planning for the Occupy Wall Street protests began in August of 2011, I was able to take time off from my job at an insurance firm and rush to evening meetings and demonstrations. As the protests escalated, it became clear that WWP needed to maintain some kind of presence in the daily street clashes and demonstrations. I moved toward becoming a full-time activist. I was the primary and often only representative of WWP within the Occupy Wall Street protests. I would sell WW newspapers in Zuccotti Park, hold WWP signs and banners, and do everything to try and push Marxist-Leninist politics within this liberal mobilization against austerity.

The US-NATO Destruction of Libya

The US-led NATO bombing of Libya filled me with outrage. Prior to 2011, Libya had been the most prosperous country on the African continent. The CIA World Factbook listed it as having the highest life expectancy. The Libyan government had come to power in a socialist revolution in 1969, and used oil revenue to build up an independent economy. The government led by Colonel Moammar Gaddafi had built massive infrastructure, including the world's largest irrigation system, the Great Man-Made River. The population had access to healthcare, education, guaranteed employment and a version of "universal basic income" in the form of an oil stipend. The revolutionary Libyan government drew its support for people's committees that operated in neighborhoods.

Not only had Libya raised its own people out of poverty, but it had provided support to the Black Panthers and other progressive forces around the world, such as the Irish and the Palestinians. The ideology of the Libyan government was put forward in Gaddafi's "Green Book" which I studied, and found full of interesting insights about the nature of socialism, democracy and class relations in the Islamic world and Africa.

Amid the Arab Spring of 2011, US intelligence agencies began manipulating dissident elements and smuggling weapons into Libya. In the name of "human rights" an insurgency was fomented. The rebels lost on the battlefield numerous times, so the USA led a NATO bombing campaign that destroyed the country's infrastructure.

The result of the US-NATO intervention in Libya, done supposedly for "humanitarian reasons" out of concern for the Libyan people, has been the total demolition of a once prosperous country. Once people from across Africa were piling into Libya, trying to get jobs in the prosperous oil rich socialist state. Now, Libyans and other Africans continue drowning in the Mediterranean Sea, trying to get to Europe, fleeing from the devastation imposed on Libya by western capitalism. Libya currently does not have a stable central government. Electricity in the country has not even been fully restored, almost a decade after the socialist government was overthrown. Oil exports have decreased, and terrorist groups like ISIS and Al-Qaeda have set up shop. By no objective measure can the US-led toppling of the Libyan government be described as improving people's lives. Libya has been reduced to poverty and instability, with a socialist government toppled.

As Libya was being bombed, there seemed to be very little interest in opposing the bombing among the Occupy Wall Street milieu. In fact, many of the loudest voices within the Occupy protests even identified their activism with the CIA sponsored "revolution" against Gaddafi that had paved the way for the bombing and destruction of the country.

The Trotskyites, Anarchists, and Maoists all spoke enthusiastically about what was obviously a CIA-funded uprising to bring down a socialist government. When the bombing began most muttered a mild denunciation of the NATO cruise missiles. However, they refused to march or protest against the bombing of Libya. Congresswoman Cynthia McKinney, former US Attorney General Ramsey Clark, and the Nation of Islam spoke up against the bombing. The Marxist left was largely silent with almost all voicing support for the "revolution" celebrated on CNN.

Even within the Workers World Party, despite our real opposition and protest against the bombing, there was a feeling that Libya was a "bourgeois nationalist regime." WW newspaper contained efforts to distance ourselves from the socialist government of Libya that had achieved so much for its population.

I saw Libya as a country where western capitalism had been driven out, and a government based on

Islamic Socialism had raised millions from poverty. However, the voices representing WWP saw Libya as a regime where "bourgeois nationalist forces" had taken power, thus preventing a "real workers revolution." When I challenged this position, arguing that Libya was in fact a socialist state, I discovered that the leaders of WWP had no way of defending their position. They would fly into a rage, because when it got down to it, they really did not understand and could not explain why Libya was "bourgeois nationalist" while China, Cuba and Vietnam were "worker's states." This was a bit of outdated dogma they clung to almost as an article of religious faith. Like most ideological topics, WWP leaders were uninterested in it, and were more focused on tailing the liberals.

Among the rank and file of the Occupy protests, there were many young people who did recognize that the Libyan people were fighting against imperialism. Many young people sleeping in Zuccotti Park tents pointed toward Libya's efforts to create an independent African currency and other progressive moves, and understood that it was the center of resistance to empire. These young people who understood the nature of the Libyan war, were often from midwestern backgrounds like myself. Often they were ideologically libertarian in their outlook.

I was perplexed as to why the "socialists" had so little interest in defending a socialist country. But libertarians, who hate socialism with a passion, could see that Libya was fighting against the international billionaire elite that rules the planet, the same elite that is also wreaking havoc on America's working families.

During the Occupy Wall Street protests I began regularly appearing on international television and radio broadcasts as a critic of US foreign policy. I was invited to write articles for anti-imperialist websites, and my work received a great deal of circulation. In 2013 I appeared on CNN as a representative of the movement opposing US intervention in Syria.

What is Wrong with American Communists?

In 2013, I attended the World Festival of Youth and Students in Quito, Ecuador. This gathering was a moment of real awakening for me, as I met Communists from all across the world. I was shocked to see that these youthful cadre from Vietnam, China, Cuba, Angola, Chile, India, Russia and other countries were not lumpen street activists, but professional politicians in suits and ties. They held seats in government, and represented millions of people and entire regions.

While being professional leaders and organizers, not middle class agitators, the Communists that I met had not "sold out" or abandoned revolutionary principles. They understood Marxist-Leninist ideology with far more depth than the various leaders who dominate leftist politics in the United States. They could defend their positions and explain world events with a very thorough understanding of economics.

In so many of the international bilateral meetings, we were asked: What is wrong with American Communists? Why haven't US Communists considered developing some kind of mass proletarian movement like Bolivarian socialism in Latin America? Why did US Communists operate in isolation from the masses, among a small milieu of bohemian, middle class dissidents? Why did American communists not present themselves as champions of the progressive

Communists around the world put forward an optimistic perspective that celebrates beauty and human achievement. Such an approach to Marxism is desperately needed in the United States as the crisis unfolds.

side of US history and invoke Abraham Lincoln, Franklin Roosevelt, John Brown, or Harriet Tubman?

In essence, I was being asked, "why do American Communists act so strangely? Why do American Communists not act like successful communists in other countries around the world? Has it not occurred to you that the lack of a strong socialist movement in the United States is due to this divergence from genuine Marxist-Leninist principles and effective tactics? Why the anti-populism?"

During this time I also visited the Islamic Republic of Iran, Venezuela, and other anti-imperialist countries, and these questions constantly rang in my head. I was seeing with my own eyes what countries that had broken out of the domination of western capitalism looked like. I was seeing how actual revolutionary movements were organized. Then I would return to the United States and look at the political left and see something completely different.

As my career as a TV reporter and journalist expanded, my relationship with Workers World Party came to an end. This was a painful departure in which I tried, fruitlessly, to leave on good terms. The leaders of the party launched an internet smear campaign against me, and worked very hard to damage my career and reputation. Ironically, many of the same smears they used against me ('Nazbol', Crypto-Fascist, Class Reductionist), have been picked up by their enemies and used against them in recent years.

Regardless, my career continued to expand and I continued to travel around the world as a speaker at anti-imperialist conferences. As the 2016 election took place, my criticism of the US left became stronger than ever.

In 2016, Donald Trump was campaigning and speaking across the country about how working families had been left behind. He expressed how expensive wars were being waged on behalf of an elite, while the needs of the people were ignored. Of course, Trump's rhetoric against Muslims and immigrants repulsed me. But I could easily understand why millions of working class Americans were attracted to Trump's message. Trump was speaking like a populist, and amid his right wing demagogy he was appealing to gut-level anti-capitalist and anti-imperialist sentiments that were widespread among American workers.

However, from the American Communists and the voices purporting to represent the left, I heard nothing but scorn for the confused workers who backed Trump. There was no attempt to engage with them about socialism or who was really responsible for their suffering. Like Hillary Clinton, the American communists viewed the working class, who they claimed to be working to liberate, as a "basket of deplorables."

The Need for Political Innovation

As my activism with the Workers World Party was concluding, I noticed leftist circles continued to become more frightening and uncomfortable. "Call out culture" where it is considered someone's obligation to accuse someone else of being sexist, racist, or transphobic, has made almost every meeting degenerate into an uncomfortable, accusatory argument.

I was several times informed that the term "working class" was a "white supremacist code word." I was told that it was unacceptable to promote Marxism because it is "eurocentric" and "class reductionist" but that I should instead be promoting the work of bell hooks, Judith Butler, and "oppression theorists" whose work was paid for with grants from Rockefeller foundations.

The shrillness of these accusations, obviously stemming from an attempt to purge leftwing circles of any threat to capitalism and imperialism, has only intensified. I have been informed that not supporting US military intervention in Libya and later Syria is proof that I am a "fascist." Despite being a Marxist who has worked for years against police brutality, I found myself fearing for my own personal safety as false reports claiming that I am a white nationalist continue to circulate. I was told that I was unwelcome in several different leftist spaces, and I have received a few credible threats of violence.

Despite many attempts to silence and discredit me, my social media reach continued to expand. Many people were clearly hungry for what I had to say. I continued to be approached by young activists, most of them from similar backgrounds to mine, who shared my critique of the problematic direction leftist politics is moving in.

In 2016, I was invited to attend the National Congress of the Trade Union Center of Brazil and give a presentation on oil price manipulation. As President Dilma Rousseff was being impeached, I spoke to a crowd of thousands of labor activists in Brazil, exposing the reality of the oil price drop engineered by the Obama administration and Saudi Arabia. I made the case for opposing privatization of Brazil's natural resources as rightists and advocates of Neoliberalism have long aimed to do.

Seeing that white supremacist politics was expanding, I began to debate and refute the fascist ideas. I formally debated Augustus Sol Invictus in 2017 just before his involvement in the Charlottesville events. In a debate held at a secret location in NYC, I ripped his racist demagogy wrapped in Libertarian Goth Edgelordism to shreds. Many deeply appreciated me for doing this, and saw that I was playing a valuable role by countering far-right bigotry with the Marxist-Leninist politics I had learned, not the politically correct "oppression theory" being promoted on college campuses. My politics of class solidarity and anti-imperialism could effectively challenge fascist demagogy, while liberal pandering could not. Julian Assange tweeted out the debate to his followers on social media, and many antifascists praised me for effectively refuting Invictus' ideas.

A community of thousands of people regularly watch my YouTube live broadcasts, study my writings, watch my videos, and engage with my ideas. I have convened lectures in New York City that have been very well attended by local people who are interested in socialism. I regularly receive feedback on my work from people located in China, Russia, Africa, Asia, South America, and many other parts of the world.

In 2019, I published *City Builders and Vandals in Our Age*, presenting a vision for 21st Century Socialism and analyzing the nature of the global capitalist crisis and geopolitics. The book received numerous good reviews. Not only did hundreds of American leftists purchase the book, but the book was widely studied in Venezuela, Russia, and other anti-imperialist countries. Leftists across Europe have also studied the book and found its analysis to be very insightful.

Under these circumstances, I have determined that it is necessary to launch a think tank that could facilitate the new, uncommon conversation about socialism I have engaged in. As of this printing, we are in the process of formally launching the Center for Political Innovation.

While I have a comfortable job as a reporter for international television and I am happily married living in New York City, I am not willing to just rest on my laurels. If anything has been made abundantly clear to me over the course of my political development, it is that I cannot expect others to merely step up and do the tasks that must be done. History is not inevitable, and the role of the individual can sometimes be decisive.

Millions of American working people are suffering and ready to fight back. Millions of young Americans are getting interested in socialism and need direction other than BreadTube's razzle dazzle and disinformation. Many are asking, "what can I do to change the course of history? How can I choose a life that matters?"

My vision for the Center for Political Innovation is a mass, socialist educational think tank that will rescue socialism from the pessimistic distortions of the Synthetic Left, and get to the masses. I meet more and more people each day who are interested in building it.

Many young Americans are ready to take up history's challenge, and I clearly have a role to play in working with them to facilitate America's transition to a much more healthy and rational society.

As Nelson Peery put it: "The future is up to us."

Bibliography

Arendt, Hannah *Eichmann in Jerusalem: A Report on the Banality of Evil*, 1963

Ciccarello-Maher, George *We Created Chavez: A People's History of the Venezuela Revolution*, 2013

Cannon, James *The Struggle for a Proletarian Party*, 1939

Copeland, Vince *Expanding Empire: The Global War Drive of Big Business*, 1972

Dutt, R. Palme *Fascism and Social Revolution*, 1934

Engels, Friedrich *Socialism: Utopian and Scientific*, 1880

Engels, Friedrich *The Role of Labor in the Transition from Ape to Man*, 1876

Ferguson, Marilyn *The Aquarian Conspiracy: Personal and Social Transformation in the 80s*, 1980

Foster, William Z. *The History of the Three Internationals*, 1955

Foster, William Z. *The Twilight of World Capitalism*, 1949

Freud, Sigmund *Civilization and its Discontents*, 1930

Hassan, Steve *Combating Cult Mind Control*, 1988

Kelley, Robin D.G. *Hammer and Hoe: Alabama Communists During the Great Depression*, 1990

Kitson, Frank *Gangs and Counter Gangs*, 1960

Lachman, Gary *Aleister Crowley: Magick, Rock and Roll, and the Wickedest Man in the World*, 2014

Lenin, Vladimir *Imperialism and the Split in Socialism*, 1916

Lenin, Vladimir *Imperialism: The Highest Stage of Capitalism*, 1917

Lenin, Vladimir *The State and Revolution*, 1917

Lifton, Robert Jay *Thought Reform and the Psychology of Totalism*, 1961

Lind, William S. *Handbook of Fourth Generation Warfare*, 2016

Malthus, Thomas Robert *An Essay on the Principle of Population Growth*, 1798

Marx, Karl *Eighteenth Brumaire of Louis Bonaparte*, 1851

Marx, Karl *Critique of the Gotha Program*, 1875

Marx, Karl *Theories of Surplus Value*, 1863

Marx, Karl *The Communist Manifesto*, 1848

Marx, Karl *The Poverty of Philosophy*, 1847

Marx, Karl *The Civil War in France*, 1871

Marks, John *The Search for the "Manchurian Candidate": The CIA and Mind Control: The Secret History of the Behavioral Sciences*, 1991

Marcy, Sam *Imperialism and the Crisis in the Socialist Camp*, 1979

Marcy, Sam *Generals Over the White House*, 1979

Ogelsby, Carl *The Yankee and Cowboy War*, 1976

Patterson, William L. *We Charge Genocide: The Historic Petition to the United Nations for Relief from a Crime of The United States Government Against the Negro People*, 1951

Peery, Nelson *The Future is Up to Us*, 2002

Quigley, Carroll *The Anglo-American Establishment*, 1981

Sanger, Margaret *The Pivot of Civilization*, 1922

Saunders, Frances Stoner *The Cultural Cold War*, 2001

Silber, Irwin *Kampuchea: Revolution Rescued*, 1986

Sorel, Georges *Reflections on Violence*, 1908

Storch, Randi *Red Chicago: American Communism at its Grassroots 1928-1935*, 2008

Trotsky, Leon *In Defense of Marxism*, 1939

Vaisse, Justin *Zbigniew Brzezinski: America's Grand Strategist*, 2018

Whitney, Joel *Finks: How the CIA Tricked the World's Best Writers*, 2016

Wald, Alan *The New York Intellectuals: The Rise and Decline of the Anti-Stalinist Left from 1930s to the 1980s*, 1987

Printed in Great Britain
by Amazon